God Performed a Miracle

A Journey from Code Blue to Home

Barbara K. Black

and

Bernard F. Black

ISBN-10: 0692279075
ISBN-13: 978-0692279076

DEDICATION

To all our friends of Pines Baptist Church in Pembroke Pines, Florida, and to our prayer partners all across the globe, we dedicate this volume. Without your constant vigilance and support, we would not have survived. Thanks be to God for your faithfulness!

FORWARD

This account is written in a narrative or journal style. It is our story of what we, as a couple, went through during 73 days of hospitalization. Both of us had completely different experiences from each other.

During this intense time, Bernie sent numerous email prayer requests pouring out his concern and asking for prayer on my behalf. These email messages touched many hearts all around the globe. Many recipients replied with Facebook posts and emails expressing their constant prayer on my behalf, and their reactions to the situation. Later, many said how comforting, challenging, and encouraging Bernie's communications had been for them personally. For example, Barbara's cousin wrote, "Thanks Barbara and Bernie, your faith strengthens mine, the way you have handled your struggles daily has and will continue to help me deal through the struggles I face. Thank you guys for your continued reference to Scripture, your diligence, your persistence, faith, and most importantly, the love that shines through you. I love you, and am so thankful I have family like you. XOXO. Christina." Also, one of my co-workers had lost a spouse during the time I was hospitalized. She later commented on how much Bernie's emails had lifted her spirit and gave her comfort.

So, we decided to present our story through the e-mail communications, some of the responses, and my own stories of my experiences and reflections of those experiences while in the hospital. You will see different fonts used for both Bernie and my stories, much like daily entries in a shared journal. We pray as you read, that the Lord would speak to you wherever you find yourself in your life's journey. If He is Lord of your life already, may you be encouraged. If He is not Lord of your life, we pray that you would turn to Him and accept His free gift of salvation and forgiveness for all your sins. I am convinced there is no other meaning to this life apart from Jesus Christ.

Eternally, Barbara K. Black

CONTENTS

ACKNOWLEDGMENTS

Thanks to the hospital doctors, nurses, and staff in the three facilities we were placed in.

Thanks to our families, Roger and MaryAnn Kinney, Lawrence and Joyce Kinney, and Barbara and Dewey Phillips who supported us all the way.

Thanks to our neighbors, Margaret and Frank Groselle, for looking after Bernie's practical needs.

Thanks to Joyce Panzica for loaning us her house in which to write this volume.

Thanks to the numerous prayer warriors who were recipients of Bernie's email prayer requests and who faithfully lifted us up to the Lord.

Thanks to Michael and Nilda McNeece for their sensitivity to the Lord's prompting which resulted in their suggestion to us to write this volume.

1
ORDINARY LIFE

Monday, January 27, 2014 @ 2:48 p.m.   Thank you Barbara and "Chef Bernie" for the delicious lunch! Everything was delicious and such a treat the way you served it. We really enjoyed being with you and your Dad. It was a very pleasant afternoon. Sorry we had to rush to pick up Hunter; we were a little late getting there. Traffic was horrible that day for some reason? Thanks again!   Love,   Sandy and Aunt Dee Dee

Tuesday, January 28, 2014 @ 9:04 a.m.   Sandy,   I took Barbara to the ER this morning. Turns out she has pneumonia. Just came home for breakfast and to get a few things for Barbara. On my way back to the hospital. Let Aunt Dee Dee know. Thanks, Bernie

Wednesday, January 29, 2014 @ 3:00 p.m.   Hi Bernie, How is Barbara doing? Is she still in hospital? Concerned Cousin, Sandy

Hi Sandy, Yes Barbara is still in the hospital. She will be here for a while, I guess. I don't know when she'll be getting out. She's in the hospital in Hollywood. Just wanted to give you an update. So, that's it. You can email me back or whatever. Let Aunt Dee Dee know. Thank you. This is Bernie.

Is it definitely pneumonia? Is it the contagious kind? When did she get it? She seemed fine a week ago, weird? Let me know if I can do anything for you. I will let my Mom know. Let her know we send our love and to get better soon. She has more books to write! Love ya, Sandy

∧ ∧ ∧ ∧ ∧ ∧ ∧ ∧ ∧ ∧ ∧ ∧ ∧ ∧ ∧

January 27, 2014, started like any ordinary day, but it ended up being the day that would change the course of our lives for the foreseeable future. Here we were having a normal life. We had hosted my Dad and his wife, Joyce, in our home for several days. During this time, my cousin, Sandy, and my Aunt Dee Dee, came for lunch. We enjoyed seeing each other and sharing the latest news in our lives. We hadn't a thought for what was to come and were really not prepared for it either. Yet, isn't that how God works in our lives? He has this tendency to "show up" when we are least expecting Him, and then He does something to alter our course of direction or make profound changes in our future.

As believers in Jesus we are always seeking what direction the Lord would have our lives to take. As a part-time college professor for the past 25 years, we have gotten into the habit of seeking the Lord's direction for one semester at a time. December of 2013 was no exception. While I had taken off the Fall semester to write a family history book, it was to be finished in December. As we prayed about the Winter semester beginning in January, we didn't sense any communication from the Lord. As has generally been our practice when we don't sense specific communication on direction, we continued with what we had been doing. By the end of January, we still hadn't had any communication.

One morning while at the beach for sunrise, we ran into three sisters from our Bible study class. Together we went to a local coffee shop for breakfast and there saw a brother from our church who joined us at our table. One sister looked around the table and remarked, "Here we are, six of us all from the same church, but we aren't here on a church project. I wonder what this means?" Perhaps her statement was a bit prophetic as soon our whole church family would become known to some specific local hospital communities of doctors, nurses, medical technicians, housekeepers, and support personnel. Our small church would be known by the love they would show to one member—a patient in the hospital.

2

THE CRISIS

All throughout January, I had a cough that would not stop. In the early hours of January 28, this cough had become so frequent that it was preventing any normal breathing at all. My husband, Bernie, made the decision to go to the emergency room. I recall getting into the van, but have only two more memories after that one.

Bernie told me about my early days in the hospital. From the emergency room, I was transferred into a regular room for testing. It was then that H1N1 (swine flu) was diagnosed. This news required me to be put into isolation with only Bernie allowed to be with me. I was on oxygen, therefore, confined to bed. I recall once trying to get his attention in the night. As he did not have any hearing aids yet, it was almost impossible to wake him from his sleep across the room. Finally, I threw a water bottle at him and he at last woke up. That story was sort of funny as we retold it later. Still, it got me to thinking about how we, as believers, sometimes are so fast asleep that we cannot hear our Lord prompting us. Then He finally resorts to a whack up side of the head with a 2x4 to get our attention. Oh, what a headache we could avoid if we'd just be more aware of His voice when He calls us. To be more aware implies we need to be listening for Him and expecting Him to communicate to us on a daily basis.

∧　∧　∧　∧　∧　∧　∧　∧　∧　∧　∧　∧　∧　∧　∧

I'm told that on January 30, around the time of the hospital's shift change, Bernie says I was unresponsive to him. Apparently, earlier in the evening, my oxygen reading showed only 66% saturation with oxygen being supplied. A normal blood oxygen saturation reading should be about 95%. Bernie was concerned about this low number, but the staff member didn't seem to be concerned. Incidentally, we learned sometime late, that this episode is now being used as a training within the hospital for PCAs on how to respond when blood oxygen readings go below a certain level.

He couldn't get me to respond to anything, so he pulled the emergency attendant chain and a code blue was initiated on me due to respiratory failure. When I regained consciousness, I heard people referring to this "code blue" and had no idea what they were talking about. Eventually, a nurse explained that it means imminent death unless there is medical intervention. Usually code blues are regarding heart or lung failure.

In God's providence, a dear couple from the church, Jim and Carolyn, was there to visit at this time. Jim went into action phoning key individuals in the church and soon the waiting room was full of praying church family and immediate family members. Of course, I do not recall any of this, but I am eternally grateful for those individuals who supported Bernie and me during this time when it was unknown if I were about to go home or not.

During the next few days, Bernie asked a nurse what my condition was. It was "critical, but stable, with a 50/50 chance of survival." Bernie began to think about the possibility of death. It is common for many couples and individuals to ignore this conversation until it's an emergency decision time. We realized we needed to have this conversation, but had never actually had it. So, Bernie was faced with the possibility of having to make critical decisions without knowing my input. Amid these pressing concerns, he did what all believers should do, he turned to the Lord and said, "She is in your hands. If you want to take her home, I will do whatever I have to do to handle the situation." Bernie recalls saying to the Lord specifically that he was not going to give up his faith in Him; no matter what happens. He acknowledged if the Lord took me home, it would be tough and he would grieve, but he would not give up on the Lord.

During these days of uncertainty, Bernie had meaningful conversations with the Lord. For example, at one point, Bernie realized that if I did survive, that either he or I would have to go through an experience like he was going through now at least one more time in our lives. He felt that it would probably be easier for him to go through this again, rather than me. One time Bernie stood over my unconscious form and thought, "I am grateful that the roles here aren't reversed, because I don't know how Barbara would cope with what I'm experiencing now. I know she would cope, but probably in a totally different way from how I'm coping."

3
UNCONSCIOUS

Update on Barbara's condition Monday, February 2, 2014 @ 4:30 a.m.   First off, I wish to thank each and every one of you for taking the time to pray for Barbara. Thank you from the bottom of my heart. As to her condition, she has shown some signs of improvement. This is all about baby steps. Her morning chest x-ray showed a little clearing compared to her previous x-ray. When she first arrived in ICU, she was put on nitric oxide with 100% oxygen. They have since removed the nitric oxide machine. The pressure used to inflate her lungs (PEEP) was lowered from 15 to 10. A blood culture that was started last week has come back negative after five days. These are just a few of the hurdles Barbara needs to clear. She is still being chemically paralyzed and heavily sedated. I won't guess when she will be brought back to consciousness. Her condition is critical, but stable. They have her on several medications including those for pain, to regulate blood pressure, to produce paralysis, to sedate, and several antibiotics. I will try to update you each morning around this time. There are people all around the world who are praying for Barbara. I thank God for each and every one of you!!   In His Grip,   Bernie

^   ^   ^   ^   ^   ^   ^   ^   ^   ^   ^   ^   ^   ^   ^

During this first hospital stay while in ICU, I was not conscious. There were a number of dreams, visions, or hallucinations. I'm not sure what was what, but the images were quite graphic in my mind and in full color. The people in these dreams were almost all known to me. The stories were mostly crazy, but there were a couple of things I remembered which were not crazy. For example, there were two women standing over me and one said, "Do you think she'll make it?" The other replied with some hesitation, "Yes, I think so." The second question was asked, "Do you think she'll walk again?" Again, after a hesitation, the reply was, "Yes, I think she will." At this point, I recall having the first indication that I was involved in something serious.

^   ^   ^   ^   ^   ^   ^   ^   ^   ^   ^   ^   ^   ^   ^

Update on Barbara's condition Tuesday, February 4, 2014 @ 5 a.m.   Barbara is still battling H1N1 flu and double pneumonia. Not much new to report, except she has had a couple of set-backs. During the night her oxygen supply was raised back to 100% and the ventilator pressure (PEEP) back to 15. But there are still more positives than negatives: she is still off the paralyzing drug, she still has no fever, she is off nitric oxide, she is being fed through a tube, and her blood still is free of any infection. Her chest x-ray has not changed over the last two days, so I'm praying this morning's x-ray will show signs of improvement.   I am grateful that her list of supporters keeps growing. We now have a couple of friends in Germany on our support list. Oh what a mighty God we serve! Thanks again to all of you who are praying. Hope I will have more wonderful things to tell you tomorrow.   In His Grip,   Bernie

^   ^   ^   ^   ^   ^   ^   ^   ^   ^   ^   ^   ^   ^   ^

Update on Barbara's condition Wednesday, February 5, 2014 @ 4:30a.m.   Here's some good news for today. Barbara is still off the paralyzing meds, her oxygen level, at present, is 70% with a blood oxygen level at 94%. This is good. Her blood pressure meds have been steadily decreased to a level of 1 mcg/min. Her original level was 7 or greater. Their goal is to have her off of the blood pressure meds maybe even today. But the best thing of all, is that her prayer support is increasing daily.

I hit a wall yesterday, so I rested pretty much all day. Thanks to this much needed rest, and your prayers, I am feeling even stronger. Also, I wish to thank John for taking a couple of jobs for me. This is greatly appreciated. We, Barbara and I, thank God for each and every one of you. Both of us are trusting Him and resting in His loving arms. **Blessed be the God and Father of our Lord Jesus Christ, the Father of mercies and the God of all comfort, 2 Corinthians 1:3 (NASB).** Who in this whole world could not find genuine comfort in these words? The answer: no one! **"...what you have sent, *your prayers,* a fragrant aroma, an acceptable sacrifice, well pleasing to God. And my God shall supply all your needs according to His riches in glory in Christ Jesus." Philippians 4: 18, 19.** In His Grip, Bernie (and Barbara)

∧ ∧ ∧ ∧ ∧ ∧ ∧ ∧ ∧ ∧ ∧ ∧ ∧ ∧ ∧

Around this time, Bernie recalls going to breakfast with a brother from church named Ed. He shared with Bernie about an experience he had had with his oldest son when he was very young. The son had a number of health issues, and it was questionable whether he would survive or not. So, Ed related that he said to the Lord, "God, whatever you want to do, he is in your hands. If you take him, you take him. If you give him back, you give him back." This prompted Bernie later that same day to say,

"Lord, I am holding Barbara with open hands. Whatever you want to do, you do."

I am grateful to our church family for the many different ways they came around Bernie through this experience and supported him by supplying obvious needs of time, and also by being perceptive enough to fill needs that Bernie didn't even recognize in himself. Ed is a perfect example of the latter. In Scripture it says that often the difficulties we go through are so that later we can help others when they go through similar difficulties. **2 Corinthians1:3-4: "Praise be to the God and Father of compassion and the God of all comfort, who comforts us in all our troubles, so that we can comfort those in any trouble with the comfort we ourselves receive from God." (NIV).**

^ ^ ^ ^ ^ ^ ^ ^ ^ ^ ^ ^ ^ ^ ^

Update on Barbara's condition, Thursday, February 6, 2014 @ 3:30am   Barbara suffered a slight setback yesterday. She was put back on the paralytic drug. She was having a hard time maintaining an optimum respiration and blood oxygen level. Now all her vitals are cookie-cutter perfect, so now her system can focus on fighting the infection in her lungs. I believe the doctors made a wise move by putting Barbara back on this drug. Thank God!   Your thoughts and prayers are deeply appreciated. I (we) thank God for each and every one of you.   In His Grip, Bernie and Barbara

^ ^ ^ ^ ^ ^ ^ ^ ^ ^ ^ ^ ^ ^ ^

Before ending up in the hospital, we often went to the beach to watch the sunrise and exercise. Many times as the sun was breaking over the horizon, I would make a video recording of myself singing various hymns while the sun rose. These were simple songs recorded on my cell phone as a praise to the Lord.

Once in the hospital, apparently Bernie took one of these recordings and played it for virtually every hospital staff and visitor who would take a minute to listen.

Some people believe that when a person is unconscious or sedated as I was, there is still the chance that they are able to hear what is being said around them. Perhaps Bernie's playing my singing video influenced the following dream. There was a movie going to be made. It was supposed to be a sequel for the 20th anniversary of a previous film that had been made. In this previous film, I had sung "Amazing Grace." Now the film makers wanted to have a revival of some sort of this previous film. And they were going to hold a movie launch party in a hotel that bordered Fort Lauderdale Beach on the sand. I was wearing my 1980's dress and high heels which I'd worn in the previous film. I was standing on the sand looking out to sea. They were going to have the grand opening screening, or whatever you call the event, for this new film by reviewing me singing "Amazing Grace" from the previous film. The media was there, but nobody was stopping to talk to me. I didn't understand why, because after all, it was me singing in the film.

^   ^   ^   ^   ^   ^   ^   ^   ^   ^   ^   ^   ^   ^   ^

Specific prayer request, Thursday, February 6, 2014 @ 11:46 p.m. Evening Everyone, Please pray for the healing of Barbara's lungs. They want to do a tracheotomy on Barbara, but, until her lungs have improved, they won't take the risk. She probably has about one more week she can use the ventilator before it will become absolutely necessary. To do the trach, they must take her off of the ventilator, and in her present condition, she may not make it. Hence, the call for this concerted prayer for her lungs. Thanks ahead of time. In His Grip,   Bernie

∧ ∧ ∧ ∧ ∧ ∧ ∧ ∧ ∧ ∧ ∧ ∧ ∧ ∧ ∧

Update on Barbara's condition Friday, February 7, 2014 @ 4 a.m.   Good morning Everyone,   Thank you all for praying for Barbara and me. I thank my God for all your prayers for us, **being confident of this, that He who began a good work in you will carry it on to completion until the day of Christ Jesus. Philippians 1:6 (NIV).**   I actually left the hospital last night at 11 p.m.   I came home, emailed a quick prayer request, spent some time on my knees, and got a little sleep. I called the hospital for an update a few minutes ago. Her oxygen level is holding at 60% and a pressure (PEEP) of 13, while her blood oxygen saturation is holding at 95%. This is an improvement, but my understanding is, she needs to have a blood oxygen saturation of at least 94%, with an oxygen level of 40% and a pressure (PEEP) of 10.   She will have an x-ray at about 6:30 a.m. this morning. Please keep praying! I will keep you posted on her condition. I am greatly encouraged when I read your email and Facebook responses. Thank you all. In His Grip,   Bernie & Barbara

∧ ∧ ∧ ∧ ∧ ∧ ∧ ∧ ∧ ∧ ∧ ∧ ∧ ∧ ∧

In my dream, the movie directors spoke with me and told me that they wanted to include one of my relative's families in the new version of this film. I believed myself to be in Missouri. There was a vision in my mind of a train running through a cornfield on a disused train track. Three of my family members who were siblings, were riding in a pickup truck along a country road. In this dream, one of my male relatives was married to someone who was supposed to be the daughter of his sister; in other words, he was married to his niece.

I dreamed that I was going to Missouri to visit this family and tell them they were to be featured in this new film. I had received from my Dad a wooden model of the house that these family members had grown up in which was located in Florida. It was a three dimensional model with each room painted a different color. I was taking this model to my relatives as a gift. I seem to remember waking up and discovering I was lying in a corn field in Missouri next to the train track where the train had to come through accidentally. The corn plants were flattened, and the house model was shattered. I was not able to give this gift to my relatives.

In my mind, the shattered house model represented shattered relationships. Many people have experiences in their families which cause shattered relationships. Sometimes the rift will go on for years. In one case I knew of the rift had gone on so long that some family members didn't even remember what had caused it in the first place.

These kinds of tragic breaks in relationships also occur in the church, and often with devastating results. A person is hurt either intentionally or sometimes unintentionally, and they begin to hold the offending party at arm's length. Everyone around can see there is some kind of issue between the two individuals, but nobody is willing to broach the subject. So, the problem festers and the ripple effect of two individual's unresolved conflict spreads throughout the church. How sad that we let perceived hurt cause an entire body to become ineffective for God's work. I like the admonition from Scripture in **Ephesians 4:26: "In your anger do not sin: Do not let the sun go down while you are still angry."** This verse is one that we chose to include in a covenant which each of us signed on our wedding day. It has served us well as we've never gone to bed while still angry with each other.

^ ^ ^ ^ ^ ^ ^ ^ ^ ^ ^ ^ ^ ^

Friday, February 7, 2014 @ 5:06 a.m. Update on Barbara's condition   Good morning Everyone,   Please welcome to our prayer list a couple from Indonesia who are very dear to Barbara and I. I am saving all of our correspondence so when Barbara recovers, she can read them and be grateful for all her wonderful friends.   In His Grip,   Bernie

^   ^   ^   ^   ^   ^   ^   ^   ^   ^   ^   ^   ^   ^   ^

For 25 years now, I have taught English as a Second Language. My students have come to the U.S. from more than 150 different countries. It has been a great joy to help these internationals who come to the U.S. learn about their new home while learning to speak the language. Many of my students are counted among our friends even after they "graduated" from my classes.

In the course of teaching, I've heard so many different stories of immigration. It's no wonder that this topic presented itself in one of my dreams.

In my dream, I remember trying to enter the U.S. illegally from Mexico. I had successfully crossed the border, and was now being held inside of a little wooden white house with an attic with glass windows all around. I was being held in the attic as sort of a safe house. I was just inside the border in what I believed to have been California. There were people that minded me and came and went down an outside staircase. As they went to their jobs, different people would take care of me. I remember somebody trying to brush my teeth with one of those little foam toothbrushes, and when I did not cooperate, I recall that they were angry and asked me why I didn't want to look nice. The implication at that time was that I was being prepared for the sex trade. I remember it was hot in this place. I could not move at all. I felt tied down. There were others in this safe house with me. A scruffy looking man was minding us most of the time.

For the next dream, I don't know if I got out of the house, or if I heard about this while I was in the safe house or if I experienced it in my dream, but down the street from this house, there was a fence along the border. It was made of corrugated steel and came down into the water. It was dividing Mexico and the U.S. In the wall there was a very tiny gap where people were slipping around it in through the water to get into the U.S. The Border Patrol agents had hidden themselves just on the other side of the steel wall and you couldn't see them from the Mexico side. So, as people would try to pass through that narrow opening, Border Patrol would just grab them. I remember a young lady with a tiny baby who was grabbed and returned to Mexico.

^   ^   ^   ^   ^   ^   ^   ^   ^   ^   ^   ^   ^   ^   ^

Update on Barbara's condition Saturday, February 8, 2014, @ 4 a.m.   First, we want to thank all of you. Some of you have visited, some have called, some have sent cards, and all of you are praying. We will always be grateful to God for all of you. **Rejoice always; pray without ceasing; in everything give thanks; for this is God's will for you in Christ Jesus. 1 Thessalonians 5: 16-18 (NASB).** Barbara is still resting peacefully. Yesterday they gave her two units of blood. This seems to have been a real help to her. They have removed her from the paralytic drug once again without any adverse effects, so far. Her x-ray yesterday showed no significant changes. I chose not even to view them unless they tell me there has been some noticeable change. She is on three different antibiotics. All her vital signs are still looking good. There has been no change in her oxygen supply. All her nurses are attending to her with due diligence; they are taking good care of her. If Barbara accomplishes some major milestone during the day, I will pass it on to you. I, too, am resting well, and I am getting plenty to eat. I am holding up reasonably well, and I believe that is because of your prayers for me. Thank you for that. So, until our next report, may God's mercies in Jesus Christ be poured out on each of you. In His Grip, Bernie and Barbara

∧   ∧   ∧   ∧   ∧   ∧   ∧   ∧   ∧   ∧   ∧   ∧   ∧   ∧   ∧

At some time before entering the hospital, I'd learned some about the tragic human trafficking epidemic that is sweeping around the globe. A friend of ours has been involved in befriending and telling the stories of victims being held against their will for these dangerous and despicable purposes. It's no wonder the following images worked their way into my dreams.

I thought I was on a ship being transported for the purpose of the human sex trade. Somchow Bernie and I had obtained tickets to go on a cruise which was leaving from Fort Lauderdale. Instead of getting on board the ship as any normal person would do, we paid some money to criminals to get us smuggled on board so we could experience what it's like to try and enter the U.S. illegally. I remember wading alongside the ship in the water and surrounding me were men with machine guns also wading in the water. If you think about it, this is not possible because the depth of water that a cruise ship needs is way deeper than the shallow water a person would need in order to wade next to the ship.

In one vision, I was inside this ship and I felt like I was laying on my back down in the hold of the ship. I also thought I was pregnant. I couldn't move. At another point, I thought I was lying on 1980's décor couch cushions and I was strapped to them. I was unable to move. I kept looking around and thinking the décor here was ridiculous. I thought I was in the penthouse of a cruise ship or a private ship. If the people who were holding me were engaging in the transport of individuals for the sex trade, the implication in my mind was that they would want to have more modern, high end décor with which to impress their clients.

^ ^ ^ ^ ^ ^ ^ ^ ^ ^ ^ ^ ^ ^ ^

Update on Barbara's condition Saturday, February 8, 2014, @ 5 p.m.   I mentioned that Barbara was taken off of the paralytic. Good news: she is thriving without it. All her vital signs are staying well within range, and she is resting comfortably. Also, they have reduced her sedative and pain meds. They moved her to a different room. The nurses said she handled the move exceptionally well. All this is great news to me. Oh, did I tell you how beautiful she looks?   Please continue to pray for Barbara. **The effective prayer of a righteous man can accomplish much. James 5:16 (NASB).** Thanks ahead of time.   In His Grip,   Bernie and Barbara

Bernie, So happy that you have received some good news from the doctors! Have updated the prayer list that will go out tomorrow to approximately 20 faithful prayer warriors. We all will continue to pray for more good news! Many blessings to you both.   Elaine

^ ^ ^ ^ ^ ^ ^ ^ ^ ^ ^ ^ ^ ^

Update on Barbara's condition Sunday, February 9, 2014 @ 4 a.m.   Barbara continues to rest peacefully. Sometime during the night, her oxygen supply was reduced from 80% to 75%, while still maintaining good vital signs. This is a small positive step. Pray that her lungs will show signs of clearing.

There's something else that may be brewing, but I don't have enough information to pass on to you at this time. As soon as I gather sufficient information, I will pass it on to you. Suffice it to say, pray that God will shield Barbara from any additional setbacks. Thank you all for praying for Barbara and me. **But we have this treasure in earthen vessels, that the surpassing greatness of the power may be of God and not from ourselves; we are afflicted in every way, but not crushed; perplexed, but not despairing; persecuted, but not forsaken; struck down, but not destroyed; always carrying about in the body the dying of Jesus, that the life of Jesus also may be manifested in our body. 2 Corinthians 4:7-10 (NASB).** In His Grip, Bernie and Barbara

^ ^ ^ ^ ^ ^ ^ ^ ^ ^ ^ ^ ^ ^ ^

Update on Barbara's condition Monday, February 10, 2014 @ 4 a.m. Top of the morning to you all, Barbara continues to show signs of improvement. Yesterday afternoon they reduced her oxygen to 60% with a pressure (PEEP) of 12, and all her vital signs remained in the normal range. Last night they swabbed her nose to check and see if she still has the flu virus. Please pray that it comes back negative. They are also keeping an eye on her kidney functions to see if she might need to go on dialysis. I will know more about that today. Pray she doesn't need to. They did find a blockage in her catheter which was flushed and is now flowing normally. That was a big relief. She's still making those small positive steps, and that's a big praise. As things continue to develop, I will pass them on to you. "The LORD'S loving kindnesses indeed never cease, for His compassions never fail. They are new every morning; Great is Thy faithfulness." Lamentations 3:22, 23 (NASB).

I had a great time of fellowship with my Pines Baptist Church family yesterday. You guys are too wonderful for words. Then I had lunch with my Brother Diogenes, thanks Di. And thanks to everyone out there who are, daily, lifting us up in your prayers. "You also joining in helping us through your prayers, that thanks may be given by many persons on our behalf for the favor bestowed upon us through the prayers of many." 2 Corinthians 1:11 (NASB). Also your prayers for all the hospital staff are greatly appreciated. "For momentary, light affliction is producing for us an eternal weight of glory far beyond all comparison, while we look not to the things which are seen, but at the things which are not seen; for the things which are seen are temporal, but the things which are not seen are eternal." 2 Corinthians 4:17, 18 (NASB).

In His Grip,   Bernie and Barbara

^ ^ ^ ^ ^ ^ ^ ^ ^ ^ ^ ^ ^ ^ ^

One time I remember a vision of Bernie and I flying across the world like Superman holding hands, and we were flat like paper dolls. At some point, something grabbed me by the scruff of the neck much like a mother dog grabs her puppies, and dropped me into dirt on this piece of land that I believed was our church property. As I was dropped, it was at night and an evil presence descended like a dark fog over top of me. I remember putting my ring finger under my arm pit and crying out to the Lord asking that He protect me from this evil presence. When I eventually awoke from all of my drug dreams, this image was in my mind. And the fact that I had been dropped on the church property was communicated to me that I was on a mission project and our whole church was going to be involved in this project.

∧　∧　∧　∧　∧　∧　∧　∧　∧　∧　∧　∧　∧　∧　∧

Update on Barbara's condition Tuesday, February 11, 2014 @ 2 a.m.　　Good morning Everyone,　　"Now I know that the LORD saves His anointed; He will answer him from His holy heaven, with the saving strength of His right hand. Some boast (trust) in chariots, some in horses; but we will boast in (praise) the name of the LORD, our God. They have bowed down and fallen; but we have risen and stood upright. Save. O Lord; may the King answer us in the day we call." Psalms 20:6-9. "Be strong, and let your heart take courage, all you who hope in the LORD." Psalms 31:24. "Behold, the eye of the LORD is on those who fear Him, on those who hope for His lovingkindness, to deliver their soul from death, and to keep alive in famine. Our soul waits for the LORD; He is our help and our shield. For our heart rejoices in Him, because we trust in His holy name. Let Thy lovingkindness, O LORD, be upon us, according as we have hoped in You." Psalm 33:18-21. Barbara is holding her own, but there is some cause for concern. Her kidney functions are testing very poorly, and they want to put her on dialysis. But, because of her weakened condition, they are hesitant to do this. They have changed her isolation status from droplet borne to airborne. A couple more cultures were taken last night: one of her nose and one of her mucus. I don't know when the results will be back. It's kind of been a

rough night, but I do find comfort in God's Word. Please continue to lift up Barbara in your prayers. "Be anxious for nothing, but in everything by prayer and supplication with thanksgiving let your requests be made known to God. And the peace of God, which surpasses all comprehension, shall guard your hearts and minds in Christ Jesus." Philippians 4:6-7.
In His Grip,   Bernie and Barbara

Bernie, Thanks for the updates, Bernie. Praying for a miracle today in Barbara's condition. Lord, touch Barbara today as only you can.   Mike and Nilda.

∧   ∧   ∧   ∧   ∧   ∧   ∧   ∧   ∧   ∧   ∧   ∧   ∧   ∧   ∧

Update on Barbara's condition Wednesday, February 12, 2014 @ 6:30 a.m.   Good morning Everyone,   "I will give thanks to the LORD with all my heart, I will tell of all Thy wonders. I will be glad and exalt Thee; I will sing praises to Thy name, O Most High." Psalms 9:1-2. Good news: Barbara no longer tests positive for the H1N1 flu. This is the result of one of her tests. The thing is, however, she is septic. They are trying to determine the source of her condition in order to attack it at its source. The one test which is still out will, hopefully, indicate the source. Pray they will discover the source and be able to prescribe the correct treatment. Barbara was put on dialysis yesterday afternoon. At first, they thought her blood pressure was too low to put her on the high volume machine. But, they discovered a crimp in one of her lines. Once the line was straightened, her blood pressure read normal. I will know more on the dialysis situation today and pass that along to you. We are eternally grateful for all your prayers. God is definitely hearing them. Sorry for such a late report. I am actually getting more sleep. In His Grip,   Bernie and Barbara

Wednesday, February 12, 2014 Father, we are asking in the name and through the blood of Jesus that you protect Barbara from any further illness and You, oh God, heal her body. Give her mighty strength to fight this illness. Give Bernie a good day as he anxiously waits upon the Lord. Amen and Amen. Lorene

^ ^ ^ ^ ^ ^ ^ ^ ^ ^ ^ ^ ^ ^ ^

Update on Barbara's condition Thursday, February 13, 2014 Good morning Everyone,   Do you all realize that there are literally hundreds of people praying for Barbara? **"Ask, and it shall be given to you; seek, and you shall find; knock, and it shall be opened to you. For everyone who asks receives, and he who seeks finds, and to him who knocks it shall be opened." Matthew 7:7-8.** The verbs in this passage literally mean: keep asking, keep seeking, and keep knocking. As I sat in a chair in Barbara's room tonight, I closed my eyes and kept asking, seeking, and knocking for about two to three hours, and I won't stop.   Most of the cultures on Barbara have come back negative. We are still waiting for one more to return. This may take a couple more days. Her lungs are in very bad condition. On Friday she will have a tracheotomy done so the ventilator

and feeding tubes can be removed. This will relieve stress and wear and tear on her mouth and throat. I'm asking for God to heal her lungs, and I'm asking, and asking, and asking without stopping asking. "An excellent wife, who can find? For her worth is far more than jewels. The heart of her husband trusts in her, and he will have no lack in gain. She does him good and not evil all the days of her life. Strength and dignity are her clothing, and she smiles at the future. She opens her mouth in wisdom, and the teaching of kindness is on her tongue. She looks well to the ways of her household, and does not eat the bread of idleness. Many daughters have done nobly, but you excel them all. Charm is deceitful and beauty is vain, but a woman who fears the LORD, she shall be praised." Proverbs 31:10-12, 25-27, 29-30.   We are eternally grateful to God for all of you who are thinking about, and praying for Barbara and me.   In His Grip,
     Bernie and Barbara

∧   ∧   ∧   ∧   ∧   ∧   ∧   ∧   ∧   ∧   ∧   ∧   ∧   ∧   ∧

In my dream, I remember seeing a plot of land divided into four segments, and I think this land was owned by several different Christian individuals. I believed a piece of this land was owned by our brother, Alan's family; possibly his brothers and sisters. This piece of land was just west of U.S. 441 and in the older section of Pembroke Pines. It had many of the same characteristics of the land that a local park known as TY Park occupies, such as short white sand hills, live oak trees, and palmetto bushes. One of the owners had horses which they kept for riding on this land. There had been a number of plans for developing this land down through the years as a complex of various Christian ministries including a hospital, church, retirement housing, and a school. Since none of the individuals who owned the various pieces of land could agree on how to develop it, eventually individual owners began selling off their pieces.

Alan was the first one who sold his piece of land that he had inherited, and it was the only piece of land which had a building on it. I believed that this building now belonged to our church. Our church was using this building to operate a 22 bed medical facility, a daycare, and facilities for homeschooling.

It was this medical facility in which I was a patient. I believed I was in a room just outside the elevator shaft. Whenever someone came up, I could hear the elevator moving. It sounded as if something were wrong with it and that the passengers were doomed to get stuck inside at every operation.

^   ^   ^   ^   ^   ^   ^   ^   ^   ^   ^   ^   ^   ^   ^

Update on Barbara's condition Valentine's Day Friday, February 14, 2014   Good morning Everyone,   There's not too much to report, except Barbara is scheduled to have a tracheotomy put in at 9 a.m. this morning. Please pray that the procedure will be accomplished successfully. Pray for the doctor and the operating room nurses. Continue to pray for the healing of her lungs. I may post again sometime after the procedure, to let you all know the outcome.   We can never thank you enough for all your thoughts and prayers. "And we know that God causes all things to work together for good to those who love God, to those who are called according to His purpose. What then shall we say to these things? If God is for us, who can be against us? Who will bring a charge against God's elect? God is the one who justifies; who is the one who condemns? Christ Jesus is He who died, yes, rather who was raised, who is at the right hand of God, who also intercedes for us. Who shall separate us from the love of Christ? Shall tribulation, or distress, or persecution, or famine, or nakedness, or peril, or sword? But in all these things we overwhelmingly conquer through Him who loved us. For I am convinced that neither death, nor life, nor angels, nor principalities, nor things present, nor things to come, nor powers, nor height, nor depth, not any other created thing, shall be able to separate us from the love of God, which is in Christ Jesus our Lord." Romans 8:28, 31, 33-35, 37-39.

In His Grip,   Bernie and Barbara

Good afternoon All,   Barbara came through the trach procedure just fine. But the best news is, the doctor said though her lungs are very damaged due to the infection, she is making progress little by little. It's going to take lots of time and continued rest and care. I received the best Valentine's gift anyone could receive. When I arrived at her room this morning, her eyes were open. She was not responsive, but I got an opportunity to gaze into her beautiful blue eyes. After two weeks of not being able to look into her eyes, this was refreshing. Nobody can top that for a Valentine's present. "For indeed she was sick to the point of death, but God had mercy on her, and not on her only but also on me, lest I should have sorrow upon sorrow." Philippians 2:27. Thanks once again for all your prayers. Believe me, I could not get through this ordeal without them. In His Grip,   Bernie

^   ^   ^   ^   ^   ^   ^   ^   ^   ^   ^   ^   ^   ^   ^

Valentine's Day has always held a special place in my heart. I look forward each year to surprises and confirmations of the love in my life. This year I was unable to have that experience, but learned later how much Bernie loves me as demonstrated by his constant vigil by my bedside. I was told he almost never went home. When he did, he would get antsy if he stayed more than a few hours. He wanted to get back to me in the hospital.

What a picture of our Lord's relationship with us. He stands vigil by us all the time day or night; in good and bad times. He longs to express His love for us, but so often we are too busy to stop long enough to hear from him. Oh, Lord, help us to slow down and be aware of your love and care in our lives.

First Corinthians 13:1-8 has long been one of my favorite passages: **"Though I speak with the tongues of men and of angels, but have not love, I have become sounding brass or a clanging cymbal. And though I have the gift of prophecy, and understand all mysteries and all knowledge, and though I have all faith, so that I could remove mountains, but have not love, I am nothing. And though I bestow all my goods to feed the poor, and though I give my body to be burned, but have not love, it profits me nothing. Love suffers long and is kind; love does not envy; love does not parade itself, is not puffed up; does not behave rudely, does not seek its own, is not provoked, thinks no evil; does not rejoice in iniquity, but rejoices in the truth; bars all things, believes all things, hopes all things, endures all things. Love never fails."**

∧ ∧ ∧ ∧ ∧ ∧ ∧ ∧ ∧ ∧ ∧ ∧ ∧ ∧ ∧

Update on Barbara's condition Saturday, February 15, 2014 @ 6 a.m.   Good morning Everyone,   All in all Barbara had a good day yesterday. She opened her eyes, had the tracheotomy put in, and later on last night, she opened her eyes

again, yawned, and shrugged her shoulders a couple of times.
Though she is still unresponsive, these are good signs. Now for
her lungs to begin to heal: I will keep praying for this to happen.
As days and weeks go by, I will be waiting and watching for the
small steps that come our way. A good friend of ours shared a
verse with us. I believe it to be very appropriate: **"Now to Him
who by His power within us is able to do far more than we ever
dare to ask or imagine—to Him be glory forever and ever,
Amen." Ephesians 3:20-21.** We continue to be grateful
for all your thoughts and prayers. We hope everyone has a
blessed day. In His Grip, Bernie and Barbara

Bernie, Sorry I haven't called lately, but trust me—you and
Barbara have been on my mind and in my prayers daily. Glad
for the latest update. Sounds like she's holding stable at
present. That's good. She's a strong lady, and she's got a
faithful prayer warrior/husband watching over her! Such love
and devotion. I am truly impressed by your sacrifice and
dedication. God will reward that because through that you
honor Him. Just remember you are never alone in this. I hope
you continually feel the presence of God an those praying
for/with you. We're all in this together; we're not just friends—
we're family! God bless you both! David

∧ ∧ ∧ ∧ ∧ ∧ ∧ ∧ ∧ ∧ ∧ ∧ ∧ ∧ ∧

For the past several months before we found ourselves in the
hospital, Bernie had been praying for God to work in our lives and
use us in His work. I believe these prayers were answered when
we ended up in the hospital. Often God has to shape us into the

vessels He needs us to be before He can really use us for His purpose. If we reject His work, or complain, or fight against it, then we find ourselves opposing God Himself. This is never a good place for us as believers to find ourselves in. But, never the less, God is often gracious and patient with us and if we will come back to Him seeking forgiveness, He will do so and then take up His work where He left off. I'm so glad He doesn't abandon His plans to work through us just because we are uncooperative at first!

^ ^ ^ ^ ^ ^ ^ ^ ^ ^ ^ ^ ^ ^ ^

Update on Barbara's condition Sunday, February 16, 2014 @ 4 a.m. Good morning Everyone, "Bless the LORD, O my soul; and all that is within me, bless His holy name. Bless the LORD, O my soul, and forget none of His benefits; who pardons all your iniquities; who heals all your diseases; who redeems your life from the pit; who crowns you with lovingkindness and compassion; who satisfies your years with good things, so that your youth is renewed like the eagle." Psalms 103:1-5. "Do you not know? Have you not heard? The Everlasting God, the LORD, the Creator of the ends of the earth does not become weary or tired. His understanding is inscrutable. He gives strength to the weary, and to him who lacks might He increases power. Though youths grow weary and tired, and vigorous young men stumble badly, yet those who wait on the LORD will gain new strength; they will mount up with wings like eagles, they will run and not get tired, they will walk and not become weary." Isaiah 40:28-31.

"For as many as may be the promises of God, in Him (Christ Jesus) they are yes; wherefore also by Him is our Amen to the glory of God through us." 2 Corinthians 1:20.

Barbara is continuing to show signs of improvement. Her x-rays show her lungs are beginning to clear up. She continues to remain in a state of semi-consciousness where she can open her eyes and move her head and arms. I can hardly wait to see the results of today's x-ray. Also, we are still waiting for results of one final culture to return from out of state. I'm expecting that to happen tomorrow. Pray that it comes back negative.

As Barbara continues to progress through this illness, I want you to know that we are eternally grateful for all your thoughts and prayers. We thank our God for each and every one of you. We also wish to express our gratitude to all those who have come to visit with us. And thanks for your cards and uplifting emails. Thank you!!   In His Grip, Bernie and Barbara

^   ^   ^   ^   ^   ^   ^   ^   ^   ^   ^   ^   ^   ^

When I was in intensive care, there were so many people from the church coming in to see me, that I believed somehow that our church was operating a medical facility with 22 beds. I thought that one of the pieces of property owned by the various siblings of Alan's family, had been sold, and it now had a building on it. This building was situated along a winding driveway surrounded by a lake and some beautiful pine trees. It belonged to our church. The church was operating this small medical facility using medical contractors. They were operating this facility in order to have some rent income to help pay for the church's mortgage. Also in this building was a home school organization, and a daycare.

There was a portico out front for cars to unload passengers in inclement weather. Under the portico, there was a metal plate on the driveway. It resembled the kind of metal plate that is put over manholes in the road. In my dream, this metal plate was covering an access hole where the elevator controls were housed. The controls needed repaired. I dreamed that every night at 2 a.m. specifically, the maintenance crews would open the plate and get down in there to repair the elevator. I constantly heard tools clanging on metal. I couldn't understand why they couldn't get that elevator fixed once and for all!

At the supposed medical facility there was a male respiratory technician. I believed that he was working for a small, independent contracting agency. I believed he was trying to recruit other respiratory technicians away from our medical facility to another contracting agency. He seemed to take them off into a small room, and I believe to have overheard him explain that the other contracting opportunity was going to be nationwide. I felt it was my responsibility to inform our pastor that someone was trying to lure away our technicians. If these technicians left, then our medical facility would suffer. We would lose the rental income that the medical facility provided to help pay our church mortgage.

This reminds me about how sometimes church members see behaviors or actions being done by other church members that concern them, but rather than speaking up about these concerns in the biblical manner, they act like the ostrich and stick their head in the sand. Then when it's too late and sin has occurred, with irreparable results, they come out of the woodwork and say something like, "I saw that happening months ago. I knew something bad was going to happen." Scripture gives a prescription for how to deal with these types of occurrences, and to maintain a healthy church, we must deal with these things specifically if they involve sinful behavior. The principle of "sin in the camp" is a serious one and stops the Lord from being able to use and/or bless a congregation.

∧   ∧   ∧   ∧   ∧   ∧   ∧   ∧   ∧   ∧   ∧   ∧   ∧   ∧   ∧

Update on Barbara's condition Monday, February 17, 2014
Barbara encountered a few hurtles yesterday which she took
with just a little difficulty. I decided to stay at the hospital last
night. Therefore, I'm getting out a rather late report. Though
last night was a little rough, all in all she is still progressing.
Hopefully, her final tests will come back today. We really do
want them to be negative. If the tests come back positive for
tuberculosis, this will mean months of treatment, and that with
very harsh drugs. Thanks for your continued prayers. When
they say this could take a long time, they really mean it. But,
"The LORD is my shepherd; I shall not want. He makes me lie
down in green pastures; He leads me beside the still waters. He
restores my soul; He leads me in the paths of righteousness for
His name's sake. Yea, though I walk through the valley of the
shadow of death, I will fear no evil; for You are with me; Your rod
and Your staff, they comfort me. You prepare a table before me
in the presence of my enemies; You anoint my head with oil; my
cup runs over. Surely goodness and mercy shall follow me all the
days of my life; and I will dwell in the house of the LORD
forever." Psalms 23. We appreciate you all!! In His Grip,
Bernie and Barbara

∧   ∧   ∧   ∧   ∧   ∧   ∧   ∧   ∧   ∧   ∧   ∧   ∧   ∧   ∧

And now for a note about the land mentioned earlier. It was
divided into four segments. Different groups of people owned
portions of the four different segments of land. One of the owners
of the land was a woman named Leitha. I don't know if this is a
real person or not, but she supposedly was a friend of my friend,

Diane. When I asked Diane after regaining consciousness, she had never heard of anyone named Leitha. At any rate, back in my dream, Leitha was getting old and needed to do something with her land. She was single and had nobody to pass her land on to. She was still holding to the original idea for developing a complex of Christian ministries. Various realtors had approached her about selling the land, and she was debating what to do. I recall that one developer showed her some plans for a condo complex complete with high rise towers and an entrance way flanked by two sail-shaped glass towers about six stories tall. The complex was to be called Coral Seas.

Leitha was a volunteer in the medical facility where I was. I could tell when she was in the building by her distinctive laugh. Since she didn't seem to have a clear idea which direction she wanted to go with selling her land, I decided to get involved with my own suggestion. So, invitations were sent out to various women in our church and other South Florida churches to join together for a presentation. When all the women arrived to the location for the presentation, I had nothing to share with them. We sat in silence, and eventually, they all dispersed one by one until only Leitha and myself remained. I helped Leitha into my car and drove to my house. By the time she got into my house, she was very tired and soon fell fast asleep on my sofa. I, too, was exhausted, so just called a taxi and pinned her address to her blouse, and went to bed before the taxi even arrived. In the morning, she was gone.

This dream reminded me of how often we in our churches cling to programs and ideas that we think would be great and effective outreach ministries, but the Lord doesn't seem to be working in that vein. In cases like these, we need to be discerning. Perhaps the timing is not correct. Perhaps the Lord is not working at all. Or perhaps there is a lack of faith to see God's purposes come to pass.

The children of Israel while in the desert spent 40 years in one geographical area that should have taken then just 11 days to cross. Time and time again, we see their lack of belief in what God said He would do for them. God punished their unbelief again and again. How we believers today must grieve the Lord when we, too, are unbelieving. God is looking for congregations that will take Him at His Word and allow Him to lead them into His work.

^ ^ ^ ^ ^ ^ ^ ^ ^ ^ ^ ^ ^ ^ ^

Update on Barbara's condition Tuesday, February 18, 2014 Good evening Everyone,   "Finally, my brethren, be strong in the Lord and in the power of His might. Put on the whole armor of God, that you may be able to stand against the wiles of the devil. For we do not wrestle against flesh and blood, but against principalities, against powers, against the rulers of the darkness of this age, against spiritual hosts of wickedness in heavenly places. Therefore take up the whole armor of God, that you may be able to withstand in the evil day, and having done all to stand; stand firm." Ephesians 6:10-13.   We thank you for your prayers and ask that you please continue to pray. Barbara seemed to be progressing well, but something happened to cause her to take several steps backward. They ended up finding blood clots in her legs and suspect one may have traveled to her lungs. They put her back on the paralytic and have started her on blood thinners. The last 36 hours or so have been a little rough on both of us. She is now stable and resting comfortably, so I decided to come home early and get a good night's rest. I will return in the morning and see how she is fairing. Good night all. And thanks again for lifting us up in your thoughts and prayers. In His Grip,   Bernie and Barbara

^ ^ ^ ^ ^ ^ ^ ^ ^ ^ ^ ^ ^ ^ ^

I believe Bernie must have been very concerned when he heard there was a possible blood clot in my lungs. In two recent surgeries he had had, he suffered blood clots after each one, and almost went home to be with the Lord himself. It seems sometimes when we are really down, God allows something else to occur that takes us further down than we already were. When we find ourselves in these places, our only recourse is to cry out to the Lord for his deliverance.

Also, it behooves us to hold our relationship loosely in our open hands and let Him be in charge of whatever He wants to do. This is often the only way we can move ahead in our lives. Consider the story of how monkeys are hunted in one part of the world. Narrow-necked earthen jars are filled with the monkey's favorite nuts, and when he puts his hand into the jar to withdraw the nuts, he cannot get his hand out because, with a handful of nuts, his hand is now too wide to fit through the narrow neck of the jar. So, the monkey, unwilling to give up his treat of nuts, sits there until the hunter comes to capture him.

When we hold too tightly to our relationships, it becomes difficult to see that God may have a purpose which we do not recognize. He may have to jerk these relationships away from us in order to accomplish His purpose. In order to avoid the severe pain that could come from such a separation, if we would commit our relationships to the Lord, thanking Him for them, then when God intervenes and wants to do something for His glory in our relationships, we will welcome His work.

∧   ∧   ∧   ∧   ∧   ∧   ∧   ∧   ∧   ∧   ∧   ∧   ∧   ∧   ∧

Quick update on Barbara's condition Tuesday, February 18, 2014 @ 2:22p.m.   Good evening Everyone,

Barbara had a CT scan on her brain this morning. At this time, I have no results from the test. Also, none of her other tests have come back yet. Still praying, hoping, and waiting.

We can't thank you guys enough for all your thoughts and prayers. We truly cherish each and every one of you!! In His Grip,   Bernie and Barbara

∧   ∧   ∧   ∧   ∧   ∧   ∧   ∧   ∧   ∧   ∧   ∧   ∧   ∧

One of my favorite verses is **Isaiah 40:31: "Those who hope in the LORD will renew their strength. They will soar on wings like eagles; they will run and not grow weary, they will walk and not be faint."** I think Bernie must have experienced this verse more than one time during this ordeal.

∧   ∧   ∧   ∧   ∧   ∧   ∧   ∧   ∧   ∧   ∧   ∧   ∧   ∧

Bernie related this story to me sometime after regaining consciousness. Around this time, I had had a setback. Bernie was discouraged. The Lord clearly communicated for him to go to the parking garage, get into the van, and turn on the radio. I am so glad that Bernie follows the Lord in what seems like little things. When we follow the Lord in little things, often those little things become pivotal in our understanding of God's grace and the increase of our faith.

Anyway, in obedience, Bernie went to the parking garage, turned on the radio, and the local Christian station was airing an interview with a well-known Christian speaker. This man was sharing his experience that his wife, who was in her 40s, had been battling cancer for a number of years, and the Lord chose to take her home rather than heal her. This man indicated he dealt with this experience of losing his wife by considering it a gift from the Lord to both him and his wife, because she was now in the arms of Jesus. He further related that a short time later, he suffered the loss of a young daughter. Upon the heels of this painful loss, another daughter was to be married, thus bringing a third significant loss into this man's life. This man's testimony was exactly what Bernie needed to hear that day at that time. Bernie responded, "Yes, Lord, I have faith, and I can do that. I can give Barbara to you. If you give her back to me; fine, but if you take her, I can go through it because I know you are with me."

∧   ∧   ∧   ∧   ∧   ∧   ∧   ∧   ∧   ∧   ∧   ∧   ∧   ∧   ∧

Update on Barbara's condition Wednesday, February 19, 2014 @ 12 midnight   Good morning Everyone,

"Those who love me, I will deliver; I will protect those who know my name. When they call to me, I will answer them; I will be with them in trouble, I will rescue them and honor them. With long life I will satisfy them, and show them my salvation." Psalm 91:14-16. Some good news to report: Barbara's CT scan came back negative. This means she has no clots in her brain. She is still on the paralytic and is resting peacefully. All her vital signs are fine. Still waiting on several cultures to come back from the lab, including the one that was sent out of state. I'm praying they all come back negative.   Thank you for your continued prayer support. It would be impossible for us to make it without your prayers. Thank you, Sue, for the Scripture web site. It surely is a great comfort. I'm linking it to this message if anyone is interested: www.mdanba.com/gods-promises-for-your-times-of-trouble/.   In His Grip,   Bernie and Barbara

∧   ∧   ∧   ∧   ∧   ∧   ∧   ∧   ∧   ∧   ∧   ∧   ∧   ∧   ∧

One night the hospital staff were moving me to another room on a different floor in the hospital. They had me on the bed in the hallway and while waiting for the elevator to arrive, they decided it was time for them to straighten the blankets and to move me up in the bed and roll me over. At that moment my brother and about 15 home school students were standing clustered around, each with note pads taking notes on how to roll a patient over in the bed. As they rolled me over, of course you know what was exposed! My brother, realizing what was happening, corralled the home school students and ushered them around the corner. I later found out, much to my relief, that this incident had never happened! It was just another of my crazy drug dreams.

Seriously, though, anyone who has spent any time in the hospital knows that all sense of modesty goes out of the window. First, there is "the gown." Heaven forbid one has to get up out of bed wearing only this thing that no matter how careful one is, it always seems to open in the back revealing all! One day as a nurse was cleaning my back side, it came to me that this is what the Lord wants to do. He wants to do what nobody else wants to do: to reach down into our inner most parts and clean out the junk; the result of sin, and make us clean again. Often, for whatever reason, we resist Him. Can you imagine not wanting to get clean?

^ ^ ^ ^ ^ ^ ^ ^ ^ ^ ^ ^ ^ ^ ^

Update on Barbara's condition Thursday, February 20, 2014. Good morning Everyone,   Great news for yesterday! All of Barbara's cultures came back negative. She does not have tuberculosis and she no longer has H1N1. They have also taken her off the paralytic. Even with all these steps forward, she is still not out of the woods. Let's see what God has in store for us today. We're hoping that her x-rays start showing more improvement. We keep praying that God will perform some miracles, maybe even today.   In His Grip, Bernie and Barbara

∧ ∧ ∧ ∧ ∧ ∧ ∧ ∧ ∧ ∧ ∧ ∧ ∧ ∧ ∧

They say hind sight is always 20/20! The previous October, Bernie and I had sat in the same doctor's examining room; he took the pneumonia and flu shots while I didn't. I've heard several times the question, "Why didn't you get the shots?" Well, actually, in the 1970s I had a friend who died after getting the swine flu shot, so I was always hesitant to get a shot myself. I need to remember that just because one person has a painful experience with something doesn't mean that I will have the same experience.

We need to keep this in mind in the church, as well. All throughout Scripture, God worked in each person's life individually. What happened to one individual, did not usually happen to another. For example, John died of old age, while Peter and the other disciples usually suffered some sort of traumatic end.

∧ ∧ ∧ ∧ ∧ ∧ ∧ ∧ ∧ ∧ ∧ ∧ ∧ ∧ ∧

Good morning Everyone,   Attached is the latest news on Barbara. "And let us not grow weary while doing good, for in due season we will reap if we do not lose heart." Galatians 6:9. Thanks for your prayers.   In His Grip,   Bernie and Barbara

Update on Barbara's condition, Friday, February 21, 2014 @ 3a.m.   Barbara continues to hold her own. We are still focusing on the repair of her lungs, in addition to that, we want to be able to maintain a good blood pressure, while weaning her off her blood pressure meds. We are praying for more clearing in her x-rays this morning. One more request is, that God will give her the desire, strength, comfort, and will to keep fighting this fight. All this is very wearing on both of us. We know we couldn't go thru all this without God's help, and your prayers. **"For I know that this will turn out for my (our) deliverance through your prayer and the supply of the Spirit of Jesus Christ." Philippians 1:19.** Thanks for praying.   In His Grip, Bernie and Barbara

Bernie, Really excellent news about Barbara. Hope this means each day is an upswing on the road to recovery. All of this has kind of freaked me out. I don't get flu shots because I'm pretty healthy. Never would I have imagined this happening to Barbara. I might have to get a flu shot next year. Bernie, you're doing so well in keeping us all up to date. Thank you. I'll continue to have Barbara in my thoughts, front and center. Betsy

^   ^   ^   ^   ^   ^   ^   ^   ^   ^   ^   ^   ^   ^   ^

Good morning Everyone,
Attached is the latest on Barbara's condition. Please continue to pray. **"Rejoice always, pray without ceasing, in everything give thanks; for this is the will of God in Christ Jesus for you." Philippians 5:16-18.**   In His Grip,   Bernie and Barbara

Update on Barbara's condition, Saturday, February 22, 2014 @ 6 a.m.   Good morning Everyone,   **"Make a joyful shout to the LORD, all you lands! Serve the LORD with gladness; come before His presence with singing. Know that the LORD, He is God; it is He who has made us, and not we** ourselves; we are His people and the sheep of His pasture. Enter into His gates with thanksgiving, and into His courts with praise. Be thankful to Him, and bless His name. For the LORD is good; His mercy is everlasting, and His truth endures to all generations." Psalms 100.

Three different doctors stopped in to check on Barbara yesterday within minutes of each other. The first was a hematologist. He said that there was no problem in her blood. Next, was the doctor for infectious diseases. He said Barbara had an infection, but it was under control. The final doctor was for her kidneys. He told me Barbara's kidney functions were improving, and that her dialysis treatment would no longer be necessary. Even though she is still not out of the woods, over the last three weeks, she has shown much progress. Her lungs are gradually improving, and we pray for that to continue.

Thank you for all for keeping us in your thoughts and prayers. In His Grip,   Bernie and Barbara

Bernie, Praise God! And, we continue to pray, expecting His great miracles!   Annette

^   ^   ^   ^   ^   ^   ^   ^   ^   ^   ^   ^   ^   ^   ^

Another thing about this supposedly medical facility, I believed that they were operating a scam involving patients' jewelry. For some reason, I believed that my engagement ring had been stolen off my finger. In reality, I actually did have on just my wedding band when I entered the hospital. When I became conscious, I realized I did not have it on any longer. That began me thinking that someone had stolen it. During one of the dreams, I thought I saw a teenaged home school student come into my room to steal jewelry. When I opened my eyes, the kid ran away. He was dressed all in black. I believed that he was the son of an all-night nurse. She was taking care of me, and her children were left to sleep inside the cafeteria. During the night, the kids ran around unsupervised. I remember thinking that the local pawn shops should be searched for my engagement ring. Fortunately, when I regained consciousness, I learned that my engagement ring was safe, although I had somehow lost my wedding band.

∧ ∧ ∧ ∧ ∧ ∧ ∧ ∧ ∧ ∧ ∧ ∧ ∧ ∧ ∧

Update on Barbara's condition, Sunday, February 23, 2014 @ 12 midnight   "The Lord is the one who goes ahead of you; He will be with you. He will not fail you or forsake you. Do not fear or be dismayed." Deuteronomy 31:8.

"Though an army besiege me, my heart will not fear; though war break out against me, even then will I be confident. One thing I ask of the Lord, this is what I seek: that I may dwell in the house of the Lord all the days of my life, to gaze upon the beauty of the Lord and to seek him in his temple. For in the day of trouble he will keep me safe in his dwelling; he will hide me in the shelter of his tabernacle and set me high upon a rock." Psalm 27:3–5.

Good morning Everyone,   Barbara is facing a major hurtle toward her recovery tonight. They took her off of the pain meds and reduced her sedative by 2/3's. She needs to get through tonight without trying to fight against the ventilator. Her oxygen supply was reduced to 40% and the blood pressure meds were also reduced. I believe, with God's help, she will jump this hurtle tonight. Please pray that the peace of God, which surpasses all understanding, will guard her heart and mind through Christ Jesus tonight. Thank you for praying. We are overwhelmed with gratitude to God for all of you.   In His grip,   Bernie and Barbara

I am celebrating with you. I have been in your shoes more than once.....Prayer is.....everything!"   Deborah

^   ^   ^   ^   ^   ^   ^   ^   ^   ^   ^   ^   ^   ^   ^

Update on Barbara's condition, Monday, February 24, 2014 @ 12 midnight   "The Lord is a refuge for the oppressed, a stronghold in times of trouble. Those who know your name will trust in you, for you, Lord, have never forsaken those who seek you." Psalm 9:9~10. "I have set the Lord always before me. Because he is at my right hand, I will not be shaken." Psalm 16:8.   Good morning Everyone,
Last night was very stressful for Barbara, and me. She was very distressed throughout the night to the point where they finally had to put her back on sedatives. Tonight she, and I, will rest more peacefully. Please keep her doctors and nurses in your prayers. Pray that God will give them wisdom for the best strategy moving forward that would provide a speedy recovery for Barbara.   Jesus said, "Come to Me, all you who labor and are heavy laden, and I will give you rest." Matthew 11:28.
Thank you all for your concern and tender compassion for Barbara.   In His Grip,   Bernie and Barbara

^   ^   ^   ^   ^   ^   ^   ^   ^   ^   ^   ^   ^   ^   ^

Update on Barbara's condition, Tuesday, February 25, 2014, @ 12 midnight   Good morning Everyone,

"Count it all joy when you fall into various trials, knowing that the testing of your faith produces patience. But let patience have its perfect work, that you may be perfect and complete, lacking nothing." James 1:2-4.

"The righteous cry, and the Lord hears and delivers them out of all their troubles. The Lord is near to the brokenhearted and saves those who are crushed in spirit. Many are the afflictions of the righteous, but the Lord delivers him out of them all." Psalm 34:17-19.

Barbara remains on the roller coaster ride of her life. They are trying to wean her off of her meds. First she is taken off the sedatives until she can no longer tolerate it. Then they put her back on them. Then they start reducing her blood pressure meds until her blood pressure drops too low and up the meds go again. So you see what I mean by a roller coaster ride; all this on top of her lung issues. I sure am glad she is in God's care, 1 Peter 5:7: "...casting all your cares upon Him, because He cares for you." I'm praying God will give the hospital staff wisdom, and give Barbara the grace (the power and desire) to jump this hurtle. She will be x-rayed again tomorrow.   In His Grip,
     Bernie and Barbara

^ ^ ^ ^ ^ ^ ^ ^ ^ ^ ^ ^ ^ ^ ^

I had a vision of people purchasing some product that was not for sale in the U.S., but one could get it over the Internet from other countries. It was a body decoration made out of fish scales.

People would affix it to their thighs with some strong adhesive so that they would look great in a bikini. I remember this woman who was buying some of the fish scale decorations for the body. She intended to sell it from a location on one portion of the land owned by the different Christian individuals. I was advised by someone to watch what happens in two or three months to that portion of the land she was located on for selling her fish scale decoration. Someone warned me that if she turned the land into a commercial enterprise, that it would no longer be fit for the Lord's purpose.

I also remember being in some beach town somewhere and seeing women in bikinis everywhere applying these fish scales to their thighs, and I thought that they were thinking they looked great with these fish scales applied to their thighs. I wondered why they wanted to degrade their bodies in this way. It was apparently considered high fashion.

^ ^ ^ ^ ^ ^ ^ ^ ^ ^ ^ ^ ^ ^ ^

Update on Barbara's condition Wednesday, February 26, 2014, @ 6 a.m. Good morning Everyone, "Ah Lord God! Behold, You have made the heavens and the earth by Your great power and by Your outstretched arm! Nothing is too difficult for You." Jeremiah 32:17 (NASB).

"So do not worry, saying, 'What shall we eat?' or 'What shall we drink?' or 'What shall we wear?' For the pagans run after all these things, and your heavenly Father knows that you need them. But seek first his kingdom and his righteousness, and all these things will be given to you as well. Therefore do not worry about tomorrow, for tomorrow will worry about itself. Each day has enough trouble of its own." Matthew 6:31–34 (NIV).

Barbara has been off of the blood pressure meds since yesterday morning, and she continues to maintain a normal blood pressure: another step in the right direction. Also, her blood work and kidney functions continue to improve. Little by little, she is recovering. She has not had an x-ray in three days, but I believe today she will have one. I'm hoping the x-ray will show signs of clearing in her lungs. Each day I pray that the Lord will make today a little better than yesterday, and tomorrow a little better than today. What a great and merciful God we serve! Barbara is still sedated and is not able to communicate. That's the next hurtle she is facing. In His Grip, Bernie and Barbara

Oh, Bernie, only the best for our Barbara. Good news is always welcome. Hang in there. Carmen

^ ^ ^ ^ ^ ^ ^ ^ ^ ^ ^ ^ ^ ^ ^

Update on Barbara's condition Thursday, February 27, 2014, @ 1 a.m. Good morning Everyone, "When I thought, 'My foot is slipping,' your steadfast love, O Lord, held me up. When the cares of my heart are many, your consolations cheer my soul." Psalm 94:18–19 (NRSV). "You will keep in perfect peace him whose mind is steadfast, because he trusts in you. Trust in the Lord forever, for the Lord, the Lord, is the Rock eternal." Isaiah 26:3–4 (NIV). Even though Barbara is still in very bad condition, she remains on a gradual upward slope toward recovery. God did a wonderful thing for Barbara; He gave her a new bed. Her old bed was very uncomfortable. The nurses had to come in every so often and move her. This new bed has an air mattress that automatically shifts pressure to different parts of her body. Since she got this mattress, she seems to be resting more comfortably. Big plus! Our major concern continues to be her lungs. They really need to heal enough so she can be moved out of ICU. Eventually she will be moved to a short term rehab facility. But first, let's get her out of ICU. Thanks for your continued prayer support. I do have one additional request, if I may. Please pray for a couple in our church. The wife is going in for major surgery tomorrow. I'm sure they would greatly appreciate your prayers for them. God comforts us so that we can comfort others with that same comfort. Thanks!   In His Grip, Bernie and Barbara

Update on Barbara Thursday, February 27, 2014 @ 1:42 a.m. Good morning Team,   I can sometimes imagine what Moses must have felt like during the Israelite's battle with the Amalekites in Exodus 17:10-12. As long as Moses would hold up his hands, the Israelites would prevail. When he would let his arms down, the Amalekites would prevail. So Aaron and Hur stood next to Moses and steadied his hands.
Thank you all for helping to steady my hands. In His Grip, Bernie and Barbara

Oh, God is good! Faithful! Awesome! You, Bernie, are a loving, faithful husband and friend. Continued prayers!
Lissett

4

ON THE SEE SAW WITH JESUS

Some days Jesus lifted us up and on other days, He brought us down. In those days when we were down, we had no place to look but into His face, and wait for the day when He would again lift us up. Life with the Lord is like this, and as believers, we'd want it no other way!

^   ^   ^   ^   ^   ^   ^   ^   ^   ^   ^   ^   ^   ^

Update on Barbara's condition Friday, February 28, 2014 @ 6 a.m.   Good morning Everyone,   First, let me wish a very happy 12th birthday to Barbara's niece, Rebecca Kinney. "God is our refuge and strength, a very present help in trouble. Therefore we will not fear, even though the earth be removed, and the mountains be carried into the midst of the sea; though its waters roar and be troubled, though the mountains shake and swell. Be still, and know that I am God; I will be exalted among the nations I will be exalted in the earth! The LORD of hosts is with us; the God of Jacob is our refuge." Psalms 46:1-2, 10-11 (NKJV).   Last night one of her sedatives was turned off and she opened hers eyes once again. Then they turned it back on so she would get a good night's rest. This morning her other sedative will be turned down slightly to see how she responds. Her next hurtle is to have her sedatives removed. So far she is resisting this. Today she will get another x-ray of her lungs. We're hoping they will continue to show signs of clearing. Finally, we should receive the results back from the culture they took the other day. Hoping they come back negative. All in all, she continues to improve a little with each passing day. We remain cautiously optimistic. Our friend's surgery was a success! After she recovers from this procedure, she and her husband will be off to the Mayo Clinic for open heart surgery. Thanks for remembering them in your prayers. Hoping for a better day today than yesterday, and a better tomorrow than today. In His Grip, Bernie and Barbara

Dear Barbara and Bernie, Barbara, I have been following your progress for several days. You are in my prayers several times a day for restored health. I have passed some of your updates along to my sister-in-law who is still in contact with some of the old Stanton North Shore Baptist Church group [where you and I grew up]. I am sure they would want to be a part of your recovery as well. We are expecting God's faithfulness to be at hand concerning your ability to get better. I look forward to the day you, Bernie, and I will be able to share a pizza again at Whole Foods!!! Bernie, Thank you so much for all the faithful updates. God bless you with His strength for each new day. In His Love, Susan

^ ^ ^ ^ ^ ^ ^ ^ ^ ^ ^ ^ ^ ^ ^

Good evening Everyone, Please read this and rejoice with us. "Your eyes saw my substance, being yet unformed. And in Your book they all were written, the days fashioned for me, when as yet there were none of them. How precious also are Your thoughts to me, O God! How great is the sum of them!" Psalms 139:16, 17 (NKJV).   In His Grip, Bernie and Barbara

A very important update on Barbara's condition Friday, February 28, 2014 @ 8 p.m.   Good evening Everyone, "O God, my heart is steadfast; I will sing and give praise, even with my glory. Awake, lute and harp! I will awaken the dawn. I will praise You, O LORD, among the peoples, and I will sing praises to You among the nations. For Your mercy is great above the heavens, and Your truth reaches to the clouds. Be exalted, O God, above the heavens, and Your glory above all the earth; that Your beloved may be delivered, save with Your right hand, and hear me." Psalms 108:1-6 (NKJV).
This is a very special day for all of us. Four weeks ago today, Barbara was admitted into the ICU. At that time she was very near to going home. You shared with us the roller coaster ride of advances and setbacks. Well, Barbara has jumped one of the last and major hurtles. She has been taken off all sedatives. This morning when a couple of good friends of ours and I arrived to Barbara's room, we were greeted with open eyes, recognition and even smiles from Barbara. You can only imagine our great joy to see this. She began to suffer some discomfort, so the sedatives were turned back on. But that's not the end of the story. At about 2 p.m. this afternoon, the sedatives were turned off for good. I left the hospital at 7:30 p.m. to come home to share this great news. At the time I left her, she was resting comfortably, and naturally. Her coughing

has also greatly subsided. After I send the message out to everyone, I am returning to the hospital. This is too much drama to miss. She will probably be moved to a regular room within the next couple of days. From there on, she will go to short term rehab, and from there, home, hopefully. All I can say is Hallelujah!! And to send each and every one of you, our heartfelt appreciation for all your prayers. And we thank our God for each of you. I will continue to send updates on Barbara's progress, but this is really a BIG day. In His Grip, Bernie and Barbara

^   ^   ^   ^   ^   ^   ^   ^   ^   ^   ^   ^   ^   ^   ^

Once I regained consciousness, it was about a day before I realized where I was and what was going on. Of course I didn't fully understand because of the effects of all of the powerful drugs I was on. I remember just lying in the bed watching the pictures on the TV and listening to the instrumental music accompaniment. It was very soothing. Even so, I still had a number of dreams and visions. I don't know what was real and what wasn't real. For example, one night I woke up and there on the floor in front of my bed was one of the nurses. She was on her knees praying supposedly for me. I cannot tell you if this was real or not real. During the next couple of days, I saw that she was quite distressed. I asked her what was going on and she related that there was an issue with her son that was troubling her. She was one of the intensive care nurses, and I believe that she saw the Lord doing miracles in my life. It was still at that point that I was not expected to survive. Even if this was just a vision, I believe that I was to pray for her, which I did.

^   ^   ^   ^   ^   ^   ^   ^   ^   ^   ^   ^   ^   ^   ^

Quick update on Barbara's condition Saturday, March 1, 2014 @ 6:30 p.m.　　　Good evening Everyone,
Just want to get this off to you before I return to the hospital. To God be the glory! Whenever someone comes in to see Barbara, two things happen: (1) Their eyes get as big as saucers, and (2) their jaw drops to the floor!　　　In His Grip, Bernie and Barbara

Here's a quick update on Barbara's condition Saturday, March 1, 2014: Barbara is now off the ventilator, and they are supplying her oxygen through the trach, and she is able to talk. In fact, she is able to talk without the trach which is so unusual according to her doctors. PTL!!! Next, she starts her physical therapy so she can regain her strength to be able to get out of bed, and then come home!　　　In His Grip,　　　Bernie and Barbara

∧　∧　∧　∧　∧　∧　∧　∧　∧　∧　∧　∧　∧　∧　∧

It became quite clear to us within the first 48 hours of being conscious again that we were placed in the hospital to be on a mission. When that was made clear, we did not question, "Why am I here? Get me out of here." We just said, "When we open our mouths, speak through us, Lord." And the Lord did.

For many years, I fear the church has sometimes practiced "cafeteria style" faith. We have chosen where we would go to serve God, when we wanted to serve Him, why we wanted to serve Him, how we wanted to serve Him, and then we wanted Him to bless our service. Does this sound familiar? Can you envision the church leaders getting together and saying, "Where should we serve God this summer? Where shall we go on mission this summer? How about Hawaii? I've never been there. It sounds like a great experience. Can we find someone that's working in Hawaii? Let's see what we could do there. What an experience that will be!" Sadly, all too often this was a lot like our own experience whenever we would go on mission projects.

Then there have been those occasions when the Lord clearly communicated where He wanted us to go and what He wanted us to do. For example, each summer that we went to teach English in China, He was very clear in His directive for us, and there was no misunderstanding or misinterpreting His call.

Have you ever just abandoned your own desires for ministry and just said, "Lord, whatever, wherever, you choose and I'll follow?" What are the fears that make us hesitate in making the leap to trust the Lord completely with these decisions? Are we afraid of where He may ask us to go? Heaven forbid He would send us to the next county to where we live to work in a drug and violence infested inner city neighborhood!

Let's take a look at Scripture and see how various characters in the Bible were called to their mission opportunities. We have the time when Paul was communicated to through a dream where he saw a man of Macedonia calling for him to come over there. This was a clear call to a specific place. This call came while Paul was considering other options. **Acts 16:6-10: "Paul and his companions traveled throughout the region of Phrygia and Galatia, having been kept by the Holy Spirit from preaching the word in the province of Asia. When they came to the border of Mysia, they tried to enter Bithynia, but the Spirit of Jesus would not allow them to. So they passed by Mysia and went down to Troas. During the night Paul had a vision of a man of Macedonia standing and begging him, "Come over to Macedonia and help us." After Paul had seen the vision, we got ready at once to leave for Macedonia, concluding that god had called us to preach the gospel to them."**

Next we have the story of Abraham where God said to pack up everything and go where I show you. Abraham had no idea where he was going; he only knew he was going where God wanted. This was complete trust in the Lord. He left most of his family except his nephew, Lot, behind. He couldn't even tell his companions where they were headed because he had no earthly idea. **Genesis 12:1: "Now the Lord said to Abram, 'Go forth from your county, And from your relatives, And from your father's house, To the land which I will show you.'" (NASB).**

Then we have another example of Paul. He ended up going to Rome because the Lord communicated to him clearly that he was to go to Rome. In actuality, Paul had no choice in the matter since he was a prisoner all during the journey and upon arrival. This experience I can relate to quite well. For the duration of my hospital stay, I was a prisoner of my own body. I was confined to the bed. The Lord brought person after person right to my bed where ministry took place. At one point, I felt like an advisor of some sort with a long line of people outside the door waiting for their turn to come in for advice. As soon as one was finished, another came in. All I had to do was open my mouth and let the Lord speak truth out of it. **Acts 23:11: "The following night the Lord stood near Paul and said, 'Take courage! As you have testified about me in Jerusalem, so you must also testify in Rome.'" (NIV).**

Of course who can forget Jonah! He ended up where God wanted him to be eventually, but he sure didn't go about it the easy way. **Jonah 1:1-3: "The word of the Lord came to Jonah son of Amittai: 'Go to the great city of Nineveh and preach against it, because its wickedness has come up before me.' But Jonah ran away from the Lord and headed for Tarshis. He went down to Joppa, where he found a ship bound for that port. After paying the fare, he went aboard and sailed for Tarshis to flee from the Lord." (NIV).**

The story of Philip is one of the more interesting ones. Here he was preaching to large groups of people when and angel of the Lord told him where to go. **Acts 8:26-29: "Now an angel of the Lord said to Philip, 'Go south to the road—the desert road—that goes down from Jerusalem to Gaza.' So he started out,**

and on his way he met an Ethiopian eunuch, an important official in charge of all the treasury of the Kandake (which means "queen of the Ethiopians"). This man had gone to Jerusalem to worship, and on his way home was sitting in his chariot reading the Book of Isaiah the prophet. The Spirit told Philip, "Go to that chariot and stay near it." (NIV).

∧   ∧   ∧   ∧   ∧   ∧   ∧   ∧   ∧   ∧   ∧   ∧   ∧   ∧   ∧

Barbara is sensing a supernatural battle tonight. Sunday, March 2, 2014 @ 8:55 p.m.   To a Select Few,   This message is being sent to just a few of our prayer warriors. Barbara has been acting a little strange during the night for the last three nights. At first she wouldn't tell me what was happening. Tonight, though, she shared that there is a spiritual battle taking place in her room. This seems to be connected with the nurse that has been taking care of her these nights. I witnessed a couple of things that concerned me. Barbara has the gift of discernment, and even though she is ill, I trust her discernment. I'm asking you all to please pray for Barbara as often as you can regarding this matter. I'm going back tonight with the Sword and read out loud to her. Please lift us both us. Thank you, Bernie

∧   ∧   ∧   ∧   ∧   ∧   ∧   ∧   ∧   ∧   ∧   ∧   ∧   ∧   ∧

I am so grateful to Bernie for understanding that there was a spiritual battle going on from time to time. Even though I was on powerful drugs, I still was able to discern when evil was about. For example, I was experiencing a vision of two children—a boy about 8, and a girl about 6—whom I believed belonged to one of the nurses attending me. These children appeared in my room in the corner on a continual basis. The little boy would open a book and repeat word for word conversations or speeches I had made in real life in my past.

This repetition of things from my past reminded me that in Scripture, it tells us that the Lord remembers everything that we have said and done as if there is some cosmic DVR recording our every thought and word. It is important that we guard our mouths and speak what is wholesome and true.

I believed that I knew this nurse and her husband from a different context before I was admitted to the hospital. I thought they were a couple from one of the Caribbean islands. For years they had been a part of a Christian organization that I was affiliated with. I was always a little uncomfortable around them, but couldn't place my finger on exactly why.

One night I recalled that I had witnessed an event that sent chills up and down my spine. The husband had gone out of the church building and stood on the church property next to the lake, raised his fist in the air, and shouted out, "King Jesus!" While I hid in the shadows watching and listening, I first heard a howling and swirling wind followed by a guttural voice that answered him. The husband ranted and raved that he had chosen to follow this "King Jesus" and that so far this "King Jesus" had done nothing for him. Why couldn't he be president of this organization that was our church? Was it because he was from a specific county which he named? I was afraid primarily because the "King Jesus" that the husband was calling on was not the spirit I recognize as **my** Lord and Savior, the Son of God, Christ Jesus the Lord.

The Scripture tells us that the "wheat and tares" grow up together, and at the judgment time will be separated by the Lord. This can be frightening, because it is implying that there are persons in our churches who claim to be believers in Christ, but in reality, they are not. **Matthew 13:24-30: "Jesus told them another parable: 'The kingdom of heaven is like a man who sowed good seed in his field. But while everyone was sleeping, his enemy came and sowed weeds among the wheat, and went away. When the wheat sprouted and formed heads, then the weeds also**

appeared. The owner's servants came to him and said, "Sir, didn't you sow good seed in your field? Where then did the weeds come from?" 'An enemy did this,' he replied. "The servants asked him, 'Do you want us to go and pull them up?' "No," he answered, "because while you are pulling the weeds, you may uproot the wheat with them. Let both grown together until the harvest. At that time I will tell the harvesters: First collect the weeds and tie them in bundles to be burned; then gather the wheat and bring it into my barn." (NIV). God has placed the members in a body with different spiritual gifts. These gifts are to be used for the building up of the body. One of these spiritual gifts is discernment. I believe it would behoove the church leaders to seek out those in their congregations who demonstrate the gift of discernment and permit them to use their gift for the benefit of the body.

∧ ∧ ∧ ∧ ∧ ∧ ∧ ∧ ∧ ∧ ∧ ∧ ∧ ∧ ∧

Update on Barbara's condition Monday, March 3, 2014 @ 10 a.m.   Good morning Everyone,   "Finally, be strong in the Lord and in His mighty power. Put on the full armor of God so that you can take your stand against the devil's schemes. For our struggle is not against flesh and blood, but against the rulers, against the authorities, against the powers of this dark world and against the spiritual forces of evil in the heavenly realms. Therefore put on the full armor of God, so that when the day of evil comes, you may be able to stand your ground. And after you have done everything to stand, Stand firm then, with the belt of truth buckled around your waist, with the breastplate of righteousness in place, and with your feet fitted with the readiness that comes from the gospel of peace. In addition to all this, take up the shield of faith, with which you can extinguish all the flaming arrows of the evil one. Take up the helmet of salvation and the sword of the Spirit, which is the word of God. And pray in the Spirit on all occasions with all kinds of prayers and requests. With this in mind, be alert and always keep on praying for all the saints." Ephesians 6:10-18 (NIV).

I haven't had an opportunity to give you all an update lately. Now that Barbara is conscious, and is able to talk, we are spending a lot of time catching up on current events. I actually spent the last couple of nights with her at the hospital. She also continues on the road to improvement. All her limbs are gaining in strength, and she can roll over onto her side. She keeps pestering me to help her get up out of bed, but I have to tell her, she will have to wait a couple of days before that will happen. Her nurse asked her if she would like a couple of ice cubes. That really made her day. Now, every couple of hours, the nurse will give her ice cubes. Oh, the simple pleasures!
Thank you all for your prayers. They are truly reaching the throne of grace. And for those of you on the other side of the world, thank you for praying yesterday (last night for us). Your prayers were effectual and fervent, and they availed much. MUCH appreciated!! We thank our God for all of you. And now that Barbara is conscious, she personally sends her thanks to all of you. In His Grip, Bernie and Barbara

^ ^ ^ ^ ^ ^ ^ ^ ^ ^ ^ ^ ^ ^ ^

Special Prayer Warriors, Barbara must spend at least one more night in ICU. She has the same nurse as last night, but

I'm beginning to think that this spiritual battle is emanating less from the nurse, and more as an attack on Barbara. She definitely is in a weakened state and continues to be under constant stress. She is convinced that her room is some kind of "vortex" to the spirit world. Also, the same two children she saw last night, she continues to see them from time to time throughout the day. I will be staying with her again tonight, also, a friend from church is working in the same ICU. I'm very tired, but I will continue to pray for Barbara. Please pray for me also. In His Grip,   Bernie

^ ^ ^ ^ ^ ^ ^ ^ ^ ^ ^ ^ ^ ^ ^

Do you recall when Jesus was in the Garden of Gethsemane? **Matthew 26:36, 40-41: "Then Jesus went with his disciples to a place called Gethsemane, and he said to them, 'Sit here while I go over there and pray.'…..Then he returned to his disciples and found them sleeping. 'Couldn't you men keep watch with me for one hour?' he asked Peter. 'Watch and pray so that you will not fall into temptation. The spirit is willing, but the flesh is weak.'" (NIV).** He was on the brink of arrest by the Roman soldiers which would signal the beginning of the Passion of Christ which ultimately led to his death by crucifixion. In the Garden, Jesus asked his trusted disciples to watch and pray for him. What happened? Yes, they fell asleep. At the point when evil spirits were lurking all around, and Jesus had specifically asked them to pray, they had fallen asleep.

We know that our battle is not against flesh and blood, but against evil spirits. **Ephesians 6:12: "For our struggle is not against flesh and blood, but against the rulers, against the authorities, against the powers of this dark world and against the spiritual forces of evil in the heavenly realms."** I am eternally grateful to my husband, Bernie, that he understands these principles and was willing to "stand guard" even though he was very tired.

During these few dark days, I had visions of our brother, Alan's, parents both dying within a week of each other. His father had supposedly died while riding his horse. His mother had then found her husband dead next to his horse. She went back into the house and set up a digital recorder to automatically record her own death and later the discovery of her body. She then baked some special desserts for specific people including the nurse whom I thought I knew from before my hospital stay. In my dream, I perceived Alan's parents had met this couple in their native Caribbean island and had befriended them. The Caribbean couple had then come to the U.S. to work in this Christian organization with Alan's parents. After Alan's parents had moved on, the Caribbean couple had stayed behind at the Christian organization. Eventually, they found themselves employed by the hospital as nurse and maintenance man.

What can we take away from this experience? Well, first of all, there are persons within our churches that are not as they appear to be. We need to exercise discernment in all matters. Sometimes people start off on fire for the Lord, but somewhere down the line, they get off track and crash and burn. We would be wise to examine ourselves from time to time to be sure we are not drifting in our faith and becoming dull. Often this happens when we quench the Holy Spirit in our lives.

The word, 'quench' is defined at Dictionary.com as: to put out or extinguish such as fire or flames; to cool suddenly by plunging into a liquid; to subdue or destroy or overcome. In <u>My Utmost for His Highest</u>, by Oswald Chambers, on page 116, we find a caution about quenching the Holy Spirit: "Despise not the chastening of the Lord, nor faint when thou art rebuked of Him.' Hebrews 12:5. It is very easy to quench the Spirit; we do it by despising the chastening of the Lord, by fainting when we are rebuked by Him. If we have only a shallow experience of sanctification, we mistake the shadow for the reality, and when the Spirit of God begins to check, we say—oh, that must be the devil. Never quench the

Spirit, and do not despise Him when He says to you—'Don't be blind on this point anymore; you are not where you thought you were. Up to the present I have not been able to reveal it to you, but I reveal it now.' When the Lord chastens you like that, let Him have His way. Let Him relate you rightly to God."

Well, to continue my dream, Alan's mother then sat down on the couch and proceeded to starve herself by fasting from all food and water. She had lost the desire to live now that her husband had died. In about 8 days' time, she, too, died. The video recorded all of her last days and the friends arriving to discover her body. The nurse was the first to arrive. She was really excited to see the special "Brown Betty" dessert that had been baked for her.

Later, I asked Alan how he was doing since his parents' deaths. He assured me that both his parents were still alive and well and enjoying their lives with their horses. I am really glad now to learn that this had just been one of the drug dreams!

Suppose for a moment that I hadn't made it; that God had chosen to take me home rather than restore my health. Bernie would have been left alone. This is a very real experience that almost every married couple will experience in their lives—the death of a spouse.

∧ ∧ ∧ ∧ ∧ ∧ ∧ ∧ ∧ ∧ ∧ ∧ ∧ ∧ ∧

Update on Barbara's condition Tuesday, March 4, 2014 @ 8 p.m. Good evening Everyone, Barbara continues to show signs of improvement with every passing day. But, she still has a ways to go, therefore she remains in ICU. The hardest part is when Barbara wants to get up out of bed right now and I have to tell her she has to wait until she becomes stronger. She had her first physical therapy sessions today and they went very well. She is also able to eat solid foods now, though her appetite is not very good. This should change because they turn her feeding tube off during the day and back on through the night. Please pray she continues to be highly motivated and fights the good fight. I would also appreciate your prayers during this time. And pray that God will shorten the time for her recovery. I spend a lot of time at the hospital.   Still in His Grip, Bernie and Barbara

∧   ∧   ∧   ∧   ∧   ∧   ∧   ∧   ∧   ∧   ∧   ∧   ∧   ∧   ∧

Yes, Bernie did spend a lot of time in the hospital. In fact, almost every time I woke up, he was there. What a comfort to see his face and to know that I wasn't alone in this ordeal. What a contrast, also, to the experiences of some of my roommates. One roommate would start to cry like a baby whenever her family members would leave. Apparently, she couldn't understand English, and so she became like a frightened little child when she was alone. Another roommate lay in bed day after day and the only person who ever came to see her was her doctor who only stuck his head inside the curtain to ascertain if she was still in the bed or not—a duration of mere seconds.

All the hospital staff recognized Bernie's devotion in staying virtually 24/7 by my bedside. He learned how to do many of the care activities my condition required. At one point, a very experienced nurse taught him how to most effectively position a bed pan. Whenever the young PCAs would come in to attend to me, he'd instruct them on bed pan use!

Even though Bernie was there by my side continually, we are still so thankful for the promise in Scripture: **Deuteronomy 31:8: "It is the Lord who goes before you. He will be with you; he will not leave you or forsake you. Do not fear or be dismayed."** **(ESV).**

∧ ∧ ∧ ∧ ∧ ∧ ∧ ∧ ∧ ∧ ∧ ∧ ∧ ∧ ∧

Good evening Everyone,   "But thanks be to God, who always leads us in triumphal procession in Christ and through us spreads everywhere the fragrance of the knowledge of Him." 2 Corinthians 2:14 (NIV). Attached is the latest news on Barbara. Thanks for your continued prayers. In His Grip, Bernie and Barbara

Update on Barbara's condition Wednesday, March 5, 2014 @ 9 p.m.   "And we, who with unveiled faces all reflect the Lord's glory, are being transformed into His likeness with ever-increasing glory, which comes from the Lord, who is the Spirit." 2 Corinthians 3:18 (NIV).   "But we have this treasure in jars of clay to show that this all-surpassing power is from God and not from us. We are hard pressed on every side, but not crushed; perplexed, but not in despair; persecuted, but not abandoned; struck down but not destroyed." 2 Corinthians 4:7-9 (NIV).   Barbara looks simply radiant. Second Corinthians 3:18(above) is a good description of her. She had a reasonably good night last night and a great day today. She had two sessions of physical therapy and she ate a few bites of food for lunch time. She's communicating very well, as many of you know that she is an excellent communicator. Whenever someone comes by to see her, which many have done, she puts a smile on their face and they put a smile on hers. We thank you from the bottom of our hearts for all your thoughts and prayers. We also thank you for all your cards and comments. They are all being saved so that they can brighten Barbara's spirit even more when she finally has an opportunity to read them all. Sometime in the near future she will be transferred to a short term rehab facility. Then I will have the great privilege of helping her to convalesce. Mainly, two things we are asking each of you to continue to pray for. First, that her lungs will continue to heal, and second, that she will quickly become strong enough to get out of bed and able to walk. If you don't hear from me every day, it's because I'm spending much of my time with Barbara. But always remember, no news is good news. Hopefully very soon, Barbara will be able to send out her own email message. Do I get an Amen on that? We thank God for all of you and we are praying for many of your requests. In His Grip, Bernie and Barbara

∧ ∧ ∧ ∧ ∧ ∧ ∧ ∧ ∧ ∧ ∧ ∧ ∧ ∧ ∧

Good evening Everyone, Here's the latest on Barbara's road to recovery. Hallelujah!! In His Grip, Bernie and Barbara Update on Barbara's condition Friday, March 7, 2014 @ 6 p.m. "And we know that in all things God works for the good of those who love Him, who have been called according to His purpose." (Romans 8:28 NIV). "I consider that our present sufferings are not worth comparing with the glory that will be revealed in us." (Romans 8:18 NIV). At present we are experiencing the most difficult stage of Barbara's recovery. Her mind is reaching far beyond her physical capabilities. Each day brings substantial improvements toward her recovery. I have to continually reminder her that the steps she took to this point were simply baby steps, including a stumble or two during the journey. Now her steps are much larger with some even astounding the doctors and nurses. But we're not surprised because we know Who brought us this far.

Presently, Barbara has been moved to a non-critical room, and may even be moved to a short term rehab hospital by the end of the weekend. We would prefer to stay where we are for the time being, but that may not happen. She is sleeping much better at night and is progressing with her physical therapy. Even with all these improvements, we could still be looking at weeks before she can come home. Thanks for your continued support. "He has delivered us from such a deadly peril, and He will deliver us again. On Him we have set our hope that He will continue to deliver us, as you help us by your prayers." 2 Corinthians 1:10-11 (NIV).   In His Grip,   Bernie and Barbara

∧   ∧   ∧   ∧   ∧   ∧   ∧   ∧   ∧   ∧   ∧   ∧   ∧   ∧   ∧

While in this hospital, there were a couple of experiences that I don't know if they were considered out of the body experiences or not. But from how other people describe out of the body experiences, perhaps mine were as well. I know that there were several times according to Bernie that I was right on the brink of going home. So, perhaps these experiences were true out of the body experiences.

In the first vision, I was about five years old, and was standing in the San Francisco Airport holding my Dad's hand. My Dad was his current age, 86. There were red velvet ropes like you used to see at the movie theater for blocking one's entrance to the theater.

They were lining what today would be called a jet way for people to exit the plane. We were standing at the end of the roped area ready to for me to board the plane, but for some reason, I didn't get on. I don't know for sure if this was a picture of the actual San Francisco Airport or not. All I know is that in my mind, I was in San Francisco.

The next memory I believe to have been the same night. I was in the cemetery in Miami where my grandparents are buried. I was hovering above their grave and reading the grave stone. There was very bright light like sunlight or even a spot light. I was younger than my current age, a child again, but I don't know what age I was. I was holding my brother's hand. He was his current age, about 56. He was holding my hand while I was floating above the grave.

When that dream was finished, the third one occurred the same night. This time I was in what I supposed to be San Francisco with my husband and for some reason, we had rented a small white frame house. The front of this house was an old porch that had been closed in with glass windows all around and there were two more rooms to this house. They were just square rooms with nothing distinct about them. There was a wooden floor and a wood burning fireplace. I was lying on the floor in the front part of this house where it was all glass windows. I remember that Bernie was in the city with me, but I don't know where he was at the moment, whether he was working or out somewhere. I just know that he wasn't with me in the house at the time.

Also, what I believed to be the same night, there was another thought of an airplane taking off from the runway and passing a line of trees, and I was watching it from the side of the runway. I recalled being grateful that I wasn't on that airplane.

I don't know what that any of these experiences mean, but all of them occurred the same night.

Perhaps that airplane symbolized the "trip to heaven," and, although we should be ready at any moment to go there, if I'm honest, I am glad I wasn't to go yet! There are so many things still to do for the Lord here! Sometime later, I learned that Alan had, "Reminded the Lord that I thought He wasn't finished with you yet!"

Also later, I learned that my brother, Roger, would often come in late at night after he had worked all day and would just sit in the room with me. I was unaware of his presence much of the time until toward the end of my hospitalization. I was touched by his devotion. Also, my sister-in-law, MaryAnn, would come and sit with me while I was unconscious. Her acts of kindness allowed Bernie to take breaks to get something to eat. Family relationships are very important, and we often find ourselves taking these precious relationships for granted. I pray never to be guilty of this again.

^   ^   ^   ^   ^   ^   ^   ^   ^   ^   ^   ^   ^   ^   ^

Update on Barbara's condition Monday, March 10, 2014 @ 9:30 a.m.   Good morning Everyone,   "**And let us not grow weary while doing good, for in due season we shall reap if we do not lose heart.**" (Galatians 6:9 NKJV).   I apologize for the lack of updates recently. I have been spending most of my time with Barbara. If I come home, it is usually only for a couple of hours in which I focus on getting some much needed rest. Since today I have a little extra time, I will send an update.

Barbara continues to show little signs of improvement. We are expecting to be transferred to a rehab facility maybe even today. When this happens, I will try to let you know. We are still focusing on two major hurdles. First is her lung issue, and the second is her physical strength. I have been away from the hospital for about 4 hours now and anxious to get back to her. I wish to thank my neighbor, Margaret, for coming by yesterday to spend a couple of hours with Barbara so I could go home and rest. I also wish to thank one of Barbara's former students, Nelsigleny, for coming by and encouraging her to do her exercise. Also, throughout Barbara's stay in the hospital, all the doctors and nurses have gone out of their way to give Barbara special care. This morning her PCA is planning to shampoo her hair. She will love that. [The shampoo turned out to be this ingenious shower cap impregnated with a waterless shampoo concoction. It was activated by heating in the microwave and was actually quite nice.] Our next phase may prove to be quite challenging as we are not sure what to expect. It will not be the same experience as in this hospital, but we are in the Lord's hands, and He always knows what's best for us. We will continue to be His witness to all those around us. Thanks for your continued prayers. We do still covet them. We thank God for all of you. In His Grip, Bernie and Barbara

∧ ∧ ∧ ∧ ∧ ∧ ∧ ∧ ∧ ∧ ∧ ∧ ∧ ∧ ∧

It was very comforting to me to know that my husband was there every step of the way with me. There were weeks when I know he didn't get more than 1-2 hours of sleep a night. He tried to sleep on a recliner in my room, but the activity of the hospital all night kept both of us awake. Whenever he would go home, he would eat and email or do laundry and wouldn't really sleep. One morning, the doctor actually told him to go home. Of course he never did. I know he was exhausted, but the Lord seemed to be giving him extraordinary strength and stamina. I am so thankful and humbled to understand the depth of his love for me demonstrated in this very practical way.

∧ ∧ ∧ ∧ ∧ ∧ ∧ ∧ ∧ ∧ ∧ ∧ ∧ ∧ ∧

There were a lot of opportunities for ministry in the first hospital. There were two young ladies in their early twenties who were my nurses for a time. Whenever I opened my mouth to speak, the Lord would put words in it. I did not know what was going to come out. The most forward remarks came out of my mouth which often shocked me, but the response from the hearer was incredible. For example, both of these young ladies on separate occasions the Lord told me to tell them they should marry their boyfriends. Both were living with their boyfriends, and one had a baby with her boyfriend. Both said, "I know, I know," as if they had heard this exhortation many times before.

Another time in the same hospital I remember a large islander woman attending to me, and when she was finished, she asked, "Is there anything else I can do for you?" The Lord told me, "Ask her to pray for you." I thought, "Oh Lord, are you sure?" And then I realized I had better be obedient. So I asked her, "Will you pray for me?" Her eyes became big as saucers, she turned her back to me, raised her arms in the air, and shouted, "God bless you!" When she turned back around, tears were streaming down her face.

^   ^   ^   ^   ^   ^   ^   ^   ^   ^   ^   ^   ^   ^   ^

Update on Barbara's condition Tuesday, March 11, 2014 @ 8 p.m. Good evening Everyone,   "But I want you to know, brethren, that the things which have happened to me have actually turned out for the furtherance of the gospel, so that it has become evident to the whole palace guard, and to all the rest, that my chains are in Christ; and most of the brethren in the Lord, having become confident by my chains, are much more bold to speak the word without fear. For I know that this will turn out for my deliverance through your prayers and the supply of the Spirit of Jesus Christ, according to my earnest expectation and hope that in nothing I shall be ashamed, but with all boldness, as always, so now also Christ will be magnified in my body, whether by life or by death." Philippians 1:12-14, 19-20. Barbara still remains in the same hospital. She was supposed to be transferred last week, but God had other plans. For the first time today, a particular intensive care respiratory therapist "just happened" to be assigned to Barbara today. She came and interviewed Barbara and proceeded to make several progressive changes. To make a long story short, she began the process of weaning Barbara off of her trach. Only two more steps remain: 1) begin trial capping her trach, and 2) cap her trach for 24 hours. When Barbara accomplishes these last two steps, the trach can be removed. All this would mean that Barbara's lungs have healed substantially. Also this would mean we will be able to suggest that Barbara be transferred to a physical therapy facility. This all would be a real answer to prayer. Remember we asked for prayer for her lungs and her physical strength. When all this happens, we know Who really gets the credit. On the physical strength side, Barbara was able to sit on the edge of the bed and to even stand for a few seconds. All in all this was a positive day. We praise God because we know He has allowed this situation in our life for a reason. Because of our situation we are getting many opportunities to share with others what Christ really means to us. We both know we are truly in His grip! In His Grip, Bernie and Barbara

^   ^   ^   ^   ^   ^   ^   ^   ^   ^   ^   ^   ^   ^   ^

On one occasion we were having a difficult time getting the trach to be capped. The doctor had indicated this was the next step in the process to getting it eventually removed. We were due to be transferred to a new hospital. This hospital was chosen because it was virtually the only facility which would take a patient still with a trach. We were delayed and delayed and delayed from transferring to the new hospital. After the sixth day of delay, a respiratory therapist came into my room. She was normally assigned to the ER, and once a week she was assigned to one floor to do the rounds. She was assigned to my floor that day and I was her last patient on the list. She came and looked at me and said, "What are you doing here?" Bernie said, "I don't know." She said, "You don't need a trach. You are going to be my project today. I am going to get the trach out for you." She walked out of the room. When she returned Bernie told her she was a blessing. She began to cry and she ran from the room. When she returned she asked, "Would you repeat that?" So Bernie repeated the statement that she was a blessing. She ran out of the room again in tears. She came back in a short time later and said, "No one has ever said that to me before. Are you sure? Are you sure I am a blessing?" Bernie replied, "Yes, you are." Then she hugged him and cried loudly. We believe the Lord delayed me in this hospital so I could get the trach out. In the end, I did not get the trach out until after transferring to the next hospital, but it was in God's plan that we met this sweet woman and were able to encourage her.

Sometimes hospital staff really made an impression on me. Usually it was the job of the therapists to teach me exercises I could do to regain strength, but one morning, a woman probably in her 60's came in and taught me several exercises. She was very thorough even suggesting that I turn on day time television and use the commercials as a reminder to do my exercises. This was a very practical suggestion, although I couldn't abide by the trivial content and the unnecessary intake of information that one hears on daytime T.V. It was like info overload. I did, however, adapt her suggestion by watching the beautiful scenery and listening to the soothing music on the in-hospital TV monitor. At the end of

each song selection, I engaged in exercise. It was only when I asked for the "therapist" to return, I
learned she was actually my doctor.

When the staff were considering which facility to send me to next, this doctor spoke up and said, with tears in her eyes, "I have never seen a couple so devoted to each other. I am going to do all in my power to get you into the best facility."

5

THE SECOND HOSPITAL

Last night I was transferred to a new hospital—my second one. As they wheeled me into the back door of this facility, my nose was assaulted by an overpowering stench of strong cleaning fluid mixed in with urine. As I have an acutely powerful sense of smell, I knew this was going to be a very difficult time for me. As soon as I was lifted onto the bed, my back was in turmoil. I began telling hospital staff that I couldn't sleep on this bed. They all insisted I had to sleep on that bed. It seemed nobody was listening to me. Instead they perceived that I was anxious and they elected to give me a powerful anti-anxiety drug without my permission or without consulting Bernie. If they had taken the time to investigate, they would have discovered that only one chamber in this air bed was inflated and that one was hitting me horizontally across the middle of my back just under my shoulder blades. The effect was like lying down across a speed bump in the road.

Needless to say, I had to keep reminding myself that the same God that had protected me in the first hospital while I was unconscious, was the same God who was with me in this hospital. In the morning I was greatly relieved when a young woman from my church appeared in my room. She was a new nurse and assigned to my room for the day!

∧ ∧ ∧ ∧ ∧ ∧ ∧ ∧ ∧ ∧ ∧ ∧ ∧ ∧ ∧

Update on Barbara's condition Thursday, March 13, 2014 @ 12 p.m. Good afternoon Everyone, "Are they not all ministering spirits sent forth for those who will inherit salvation?" Hebrews 1:14 (NKJV). "Fear not, for I am with you; be not dismayed, for I am your God. I will strengthen you, yes, I will help you, I will uphold you with My righteous right hand." Isaiah 41:10 (NKJV). Barbara has spent her first night in her new home, (for the time being), and was, at first, a little apprehensive. The reason for Barbara's anxiety was because most of the people we spoke with about this particular facility gave us grim reviews, and told us we should try to send her any place else. But there was nowhere else to send her, so we knew that this was the place God wanted her to be. Turns out that two of Barbara's close friends "just happened" to work there and have put out the word to everyone at the facility that Barbara is a special patient. Yes, this room is substantially smaller, along with some other adjustments to be made, but the staff is top notch and will take very good care of Barbara. We thank all of you for all your thoughts and prayers. In His Grip, Bernie and Barbara

∧   ∧   ∧   ∧   ∧   ∧   ∧   ∧   ∧   ∧   ∧   ∧   ∧   ∧   ∧

Even though I was in the hospital and on pain killing drugs which caused crazy dreams, God did have a sense of humor and allowed me to get a laugh out of some of my dreams. For example, my pastor is what you could call a "macho Cuban." One day when he came to visit, he had to put on a gown and mask which made him look a bit like he was wearing a dress! I had a good laugh about that. In the night then, I had a vision of him singing in a mariachi band wearing a straw hat with beads hanging from the brim and a couple of woven fish made from straw dangling from the hat band similar to the image of "Minnie Pearl." This dream was so real I actually asked him the next morning if he had a straw hat with beads. Of course he didn't!

I am so grateful for my pastor. He has gifts of mercy and is always available whenever someone is sick and has a need in their lives. Even months afterwards, he continues to call and pray. What a privilege to be under his leadership.

Another funny dream involved our friends, Rick and Isabel, and Isabel's parents, Maria and Victor. In this dream, they had come down to visit from Jacksonville, and they rode a motorcycle all the way down. I recalled that they looked about 20 years younger than their present age. When they arrived, the first thing they did was take Victor on the back of the motorcycle with Rick. Victor also looked about 40 years younger than his present age. He was dressed in shorts, a Hawaiian print shirt, straw hat, and had on mirrored sunglasses. Maria kept remarking that he was looking suave! He kept repeating that he was suave. Whenever I recalled this dream, it brought a smile to my face. Good friends are a treasure and for that I am grateful. Also, the fact that they looked considerably younger in my dream that their current ages was a reminder to me that one day we will be done with these aging bodies and will receive new bodies in Heaven. I like to think these new bodies will be perfect; no imperfections or illnesses to worry about. I also take comfort in the fact that, **"…to be absent from the body [is to be] present with the Lord." 2 Corinthians 5:8.**

^　^　^　^　^　^　^　^　^　^　^　^　^　^　^

Update on Barbara's condition Monday, March 17, 2014 @ 11 a.m. "But He needed to go through Samaria." John 4:4 (NKJV). "Jesus said to him, (Peter), 'Feed My sheep. Most assuredly, I say to you, when you were younger, you girded yourself and walked where you wished; but when you are old, you will stretch out your hands, and another will gird you and carry you where you do not wish." John 21:17-18 (NKJV). Top of the morning to you all, Happy St. Patrick's Day! Barbara continues her gradual forward progress. A couple of nights were a little rough on her, but she made it through them. Every day she shows signs of strengthening physically. As I write this memo, she is in a physical therapy session. Maybe, in two or three days, she will have the trach removed. This would be another major hurtle. This also means that her lungs are steadily improving. We're hoping by the end of the week she will be able to stand on her own. You can only imagine the exceeding joy this would bring. In our next update, we may have a little surprise for all of you. We'll see how it works out. Thanks from the bottom of our hearts for all your thoughts and prayers!! In His Grip, Bernie and Barbara

^ ^ ^ ^ ^ ^ ^ ^ ^ ^ ^ ^ ^ ^ ^

On another occasion, a respiratory therapist came into the room. He saw me laying in the bed and he exclaimed, "Hello, Mrs. Black." He had been one of my ESOL students ten years before at Miami Dade College. Now he was my respiratory technologist. I remembered him, probably because he had an unusual name. It is always important to remember the student's names. And that has been my attempt throughout 25 years of teaching ESOL. I told him that now he was going to teach me. What a humbling experience. It was also difficult for him, because his culture required him to respect the teacher and keep at arm's distance as if the teacher is on a pedestal. Now his job demanded that he put aside that cultural practice and serve and touch me. This reminded me that Jesus did not allow cultural practices to interfere with his ministry toward others. He washed his disciples' feet. **John 13:4-5: "So he got up from the meal took off his outer clothing, and wrapped a towel around his waist. After that, he poured water into a basin and began to wash his disciples' feet, drying them with the towel that was wrapped around him." (NIV).** Foot washing was a job reserved for the lowest servant in the household. Here Jesus is the Master and He was taking on the role of the lowest servant. What a shock to the disciples sense of culture. Also, He allowed a sinful woman to touch him. **Luke 7:36-38: "When one of the Pharisees invited Jesus to have dinner with him, he went to the Pharisee's house and reclined at the table.**

A woman in that town who lived a sinful life learned that Jesus was eating at the Pharisee's house, so she came there with an alabaster jar of perfume. As she stood behind him at his feet weeping, she began to wet his feet with her tears. Then she wiped them with her hair, kissed them and poured perfume on them." (NIV). There are many, many references of Christ crossing cultural barriers to minister to a person's soul.

∧   ∧   ∧   ∧   ∧   ∧   ∧   ∧   ∧   ∧   ∧   ∧   ∧   ∧   ∧

Update on Barbara's condition Tuesday, March 18, 2014 @ 8:30 p.m.   Good evening Everyone,   First, we'd like to wish Bernie's sister, Barbara, a very Happy Birthday. Second, we'd like to thank everyone who has visited, sent cards, provided meals, brought or sent flowers, (including a get well message from "afar"), or has sent greetings and encouragement via email or Facebook. All your kindnesses have touched our hearts and helped to strengthen us.   "Husbands, love your wives, just as Christ also loved the church and gave Himself for her...So husbands ought to love their own wives as their own bodies; he who loves his wife loves himself." Ephesians 5:25, 28 (NKJV).   "And He, (Jesus) answered and said to them, 'Have you not read that He who made them at the beginning made them male and female,' and said, 'For this reason a man shall leave his father and mother and shall be joined to his wife, and the two shall become one flesh.'" Matthew 19:4-6 (NKJV).   Today we leaped another hurtle, Barbara had her trach removed. Hallelujah!! Today during her physical therapy, she was able to stand, with assistance, four times for a few seconds each time. Her strength is gradually returning. She will be evaluated tomorrow to see if her PEG, feeding tube, can be removed. All this is very positive, but we are still on the roller coaster ride of our lives. We have come to consider the circumstances we are in to be a great adventure. **"Not that I speak in regard to need, for I have learned in whatever state I am, to be content." Philippians 4:11 (NKJV).** Thank you for continuing to think about us and to pray for us.   In His Grip, Bernie and Barbara

∧ ∧ ∧ ∧ ∧ ∧ ∧ ∧ ∧ ∧ ∧ ∧ ∧ ∧ ∧

The opportunities for ministry here are endless. It seems that everyone who enters my room has a need. It also seemed that a pattern was becoming evident. Whenever I had a particularly difficult sleepless night, for whatever reason, inevitably, the next day, someone would appear in my room with a definite need for the Lord. For example, on one of the first nights in the second hospital, I asked for one of the pain medications to be removed. Unknown to me, they removed all the medications in one fell swoop. That night was horrible. I had no idea how much the pain medication had affected me, nor how much withdrawal I would have to go through. It was all withdrawn in one night. I could not sleep. I could not lay still. My mind was racing. The next morning the Lord brought a young lady to my bed. We engaged in conversation. I asked her if she was a Cristian. She said something to the effect of, "I'm becoming one or I'm part way there." In my mind there came the vision of straddling a fence. I asked her what she meant. She responded with a list of requirements that she felt she had to meet in order to be a Christian. They all revolved around certain behaviors. I told her that she could know that she was a Christian and that she could know for certain she would go to heaven. Of course, as always happened, she was called away at that moment. The enemy was hard at work preventing almost every attempt to share Christ with hospital staff. Later that evening my brother came to visit after work. We called my husband at home and he gave all of the Scriptures to my brother for the plan of salvation. We made a list, and the next day we were able to give it to the young lady. I told her we would be praying for her that day. The next day when she came in, she had a glow about her and she seemed excited. She did not express anything to us about whether she had made a commitment to Christ or not. I know that the Scriptures were clear, and if she took the opportunity to read them, I believe she could have understood clearly what is required to enter that relationship with Christ.

It is as if God had put us in the hospital to take the "spiritual temperature" of our community. Through talking to many people, we have made some disturbing conclusions: the African Americans, islanders, and Hispanics generally welcomed our comments and talk about the Lord, while everyone from our own Anglo culture tuned out and turned off whatever we had to say of a spiritual nature unless they already were believers in Christ.

^ ^ ^ ^ ^ ^ ^ ^ ^ ^ ^ ^ ^ ^ ^

Update on Barbara's Condition Monday, March 24, 2014 @ 1 p.m.   Good afternoon Everyone, "I waited patiently for the LORD; He turned to me and heard my cry. He lifted me out of the slimy pit, out of the mud and mire; He set my feet on a rock and gave me a firm place to stand. He put a new song in my mouth, a hymn of praise to our God. Many will see and fear and put their trust in the LORD. Blessed is the man who makes the LORD his trust, who does not look to the proud, to those who turn aside to false gods. Many, O LORD my God, are the wonders You have done. The things You planned for us no one can recount to You; were I to speak and tell of them, they would be too many to declare." Psalm 40:1-5 (NKJV). At this point in Barbara's recovery, she has accomplished almost all of the healing process. No more trach, no more PEG (feeding tube), and she only uses a small amount of oxygen at night while she is sleeping. While, every day she shows signs of strengthening, she still can't get out of bed or walk. And, she can only stand, with assistance, for only short periods of time. So, the next phase of her recovery process is to gain back her strength. This could still take quite a bit of time. If God choses to shorten the process, she will be coming home way sooner than expected.   Thanks for your continued thoughts and prayers! In His Grip,   Bernie and Barbara

∧   ∧   ∧   ∧   ∧   ∧   ∧   ∧   ∧   ∧   ∧   ∧   ∧   ∧   ∧

Physical therapy began in earnest in this hospital. One of my good friends from church was a therapist here. She inspired confidence in me as she patiently helped me to stand for the first time and to walk again. It had been more than two months since I was even able to sit upright in bed. The exhilaration of standing and feeling the blood rushing to my head was such a joy to experience. Whenever I was taken to physical therapy, I would go into my "international teacher mode" greeting everyone I saw and smiling at them. Some people were quite beaten down and discouraged over their various conditions. I believe a person's own attitude contributes greatly to their recovery and sense of well-being. So, instead of lapsing into the same, 'woe is me' attitude, I tried to do something to lift everyone's spirits. For example, a couple of the therapists were really good dancers. Whenever the therapy room music choices had a Caribbean flair, I'd request these therapists to dance. Everyone loved seeing them perform and all the patients laughed. I know that laughing is good medicine. Eventually, the therapists requested we move with the music which is one of the only occasions we actually exercised our upper bodies. I am so grateful for my therapists' persistence in making me succeed with regaining my physical strength.

Music has always been very special to me, helping me communicate sometimes what is difficult to verbalize. So, when I was in a therapy session, the song, "You Raise Me Up" was playing and I just reflected on my husband and sat there crying my eyes out. The lyrics that particularly spoke to me were: "You raise me up, so I can stand on mountains, You raise me up to walk on stormy seas; I am strong when I am on your shoulders. You raise me up to more than I can be."

6
ON THE MEND

Update on Barbara's condition Wednesday, March 26, 2014 @ 10 p.m.   Good evening Everyone,   First, let's wish a happy birthday to Barbara's brother, Roger.   **"But seek first the kingdom of God and His righteousness, and all these things will be added to you. Therefore do not be anxious about tomorrow, for tomorrow will be anxious for itself. Sufficient for the day is its own trouble." Matthew 6:33-34 (ESV).**   We have come to another crossroad. It's time for Barbara to leave the hospital and go to a rehab facility. We have a particular facility in mind, but we are experiencing some opposition. We trust that the LORD will provide the perfect place according to His will and our need. We are praying that God will give us the wisdom to make the right decision. We would appreciate your prayers regarding this matter.   Barbara is actually walking with a walker. She can stand with minimal help, and she's gaining new strength every day. One of the physical therapists said today that Barbara was "a miracle." In His Grip, Barbara and Bernie

Barbara Black, you are a miracle. God does have many things for you to do and to witness. Bernie gets a special jewel in his crown for all the care giving and prayer.   Glenda

∧ ∧ ∧ ∧ ∧ ∧ ∧ ∧ ∧ ∧ ∧ ∧ ∧ ∧ ∧

Even though I'm told I was making progress, there were some nights when I felt I was unable to see another day. It was a dark feeling. Bernie would try to encourage me telling me all the things we would do when I got out of there, but I just couldn't see myself living another day. One night when I was feeling this way, I realized that I'd never said some things to my family about how I really feel about them. So, I got on the phone to my Dad and then to my brother. I said those things that everyone wishes they would say some day, but often never get around to actually saying them. I felt such relief after those phone conversations that I drifted into peaceful sleep and awoke the next morning with the heaviness lifted.

About a week later, I had another episode where I thought I wouldn't live to see the morning. This time I realized that I needed to communicate just how much my husband means to me. So, after doing so, I again went to peaceful sleep and woke refreshed in the morning.

Perhaps a year earlier, one day I was walking in a strip mall on my way to the supermarket when the Lord just said to me, "Are you ready to come home?" This question was seemingly out of the blue, and so I responded, "Yes, I am, but I will miss some things like the people in my life and the fact that I've not been to Ireland." What a response to the God of the universe! Here He was asking me to verbalize whether or not He Himself was, in fact, enough for me. My response, when I reflect on it now, was pitiful. Of course most of us fear death. As believers, I think we often fear the methods in which we will die because this is unknown and may be painful, though I believe we do not fear the state of being dead because, in fact, we will be in the presence of the God of the universe, and that is nothing to fear at all; on the contrary, it is something we should long for.

^   ^   ^   ^   ^   ^   ^   ^   ^   ^   ^   ^   ^   ^   ^

Special update on Barbara's condition Thursday, March 27, 2014   Good morning Everyone,   In our last message, we mentioned that we are hoping to get Barbara into a particular rehab facility. Now we would like to request prayer that God would place Barbara into this facility. We understand that wherever we go, that's the place God wants us to be. But until we are actually transported, we are asking God to direct us to this one particular facility. Thanks for praying. In His Grip, Barbara and Bernie

^ ^ ^ ^ ^ ^ ^ ^ ^ ^ ^ ^ ^ ^ ^

Update on Barbara's condition Friday, March 28, 2014 @ 12 p.m.   Good afternoon Everyone, **"Now to Him who is able to do immeasurably more than all we ask or imagine, according to His power that is at work in us, to Him be glory in the church and in Jesus Christ throughout all generations, for ever and ever! Amen." Ephesians 3:20-21.**   Thanks to all who prayed and to God who answers prayer according to His will. God granted our request. We are being transferred today at 4 p.m. to a rehab facility in Hollywood. If all goes well, Barbara may be coming home in about two weeks. Today, Friday, March 28, 2014, marks the two month anniversary of Barbara's hospitalization. The LORD has truly led and guided us through this whole adventure. We count it all joy! In no time at all Barbara will be sending a very special update to all of you. When we think about the multitude of people who have lifted us up in their thoughts and prayers, we weep with gratitude for you and give all the glory to our God who has never let us slip from His grip.   In His Grip, Barbara and Bernie

∧ ∧ ∧ ∧ ∧ ∧ ∧ ∧ ∧ ∧ ∧ ∧ ∧ ∧ ∧

I was transferred in the early evening to the third hospital—a rehabilitation facility. When they wheeled me into the front door, I felt physically a muzzle being put on my mouth. This sort of surprised me because in the previous two facilities, every time I would open my mouth, the word of the Lord came out. So, this sensation was something unexpected. When I arrived at my new room, I was so surprised to see the two different requests made to the Lord had been granted in the one room. I had a private room and a window! What an unexpected joy. The first nurse I met had a lanyard around her neck that said, "I love Jesus." It seemed that everyone I met at first was a believer and they were encouraging me. So, for the first day or so, I realized what this muzzle vision had been about—it was my time to be refreshed and to receive from other believers. This much needed rest was a good thing, too, because it was not long before ministry opportunities began again in earnest.

Whatever facility we were in, we always made a point to learn our attendants' names and to greet each one as they entered my room. The food servers were no exception. In fact, we developed such a relationship with them, they began "making up excuses" to leave us extra food for Bernie. For example, one day they brought one each of the entrees and said, "We didn't know which one you wanted, so we brought one of each." We saw these acts of kindness as the Lord supplying our needs. He can use whatever method He wishes to supply our needs.

∧ ∧ ∧ ∧ ∧ ∧ ∧ ∧ ∧ ∧ ∧ ∧ ∧ ∧ ∧

Update on Barbara's condition Wednesday, April 2, 2014 @ 10:30 p.m. Good evening Everyone, "I will not die but live, and will proclaim what the LORD has done." Psalms 118:17.

"Do not merely listen to the word, and so deceive yourselves.
Do what it says. Anyone who listens to the word but does not
do what it says is like a man who looks at his face in a mirror and,
after looking at himself, goes away and immediately forgets what
he looks like. But the man who looks intently into the perfect law
that gives freedom, and continues to do this, not forgetting what
he has heard, but doing it—he will be blessed in what he does."
James 1:22-25.   Barbara continues to improve in every
way. I was able to view her latest x-ray and saw that her lungs are
almost totally healed. There is still a small amount of haze, but
when a previous x-ray was put alongside the latest one, the
difference was like night and day. She is no longer on oxygen
and her breathing treatments have been stopped.

Every day she is showing signs of strengthening physically.
Some of the highlights would include: standing, getting in and
out of bed, dressing herself, eating meals unassisted, and
walking with a walker. Her scheduled discharge date is
Thursday, April 10, but the way she is improving, she will come
home sooner. But the greatest gain is the way God is using her
to influence the lives of others. She's touching the lives of
patients, nurses, therapists, friends and family who come to visit,
and even family members of other patients. Since January 28,
2014, we have been on a mission project. We didn't choose this
project, nevertheless, we thank God for redirecting our lives to
correspond to His agenda. Even after Barbara has fully
recovered from this illness, our desire is to remain on mission with
God.   "Do everything without complaining or arguing, so that
you may become blameless and pure, children of God without

fault in a crooked and depraved generation, in which you shine like stars in the universe as you hold out the word of life."
Philippians 2:14-16.   In His Grip,   Barbara and Bernie

^   ^   ^   ^   ^   ^   ^   ^   ^   ^   ^   ^   ^   ^   ^

Here's one day of ministry opportunities for an example. Early in the morning, I was taken for a chest x-ray. The young technician was wheeling me out to a hallway to wait for transport back to my room. The Lord said to me, "Tell her that I love her." So, I did. Her eyes got big as saucers and she simply said, "Oh, thank you."

Next, I went to a group exercise class and Bernie attended with me. While there, the CD player which provided the music by which we exercised, suddenly quit working. The therapist didn't know what to do, so I suggested someone sing. She replied, "O.K., you sing." I said that Bernie would sing. Then she said, "O.K., you sing together." We sang "The Love of God" in harmony. When we finished, one patient was crying her eyes out and said that she had really needed to hear that song on that day.

After the therapy session, the therapist wheeled me back to my room. As we were going along, the conversation turned to the Lord. She kept on saying, "You don't understand. It's too bad." I kept replying that nothing was too bad to be forgiven for. She only repeated again and again, "It's too bad." Then the Lord spoke to me and said, "Be quiet and listen to her." So, she began to tell me what she considered so bad. At the moment she revealed her issue to me, her pager went off and she had to leave. I tried numerous times to reconnect with her during the remainder of my stay, but to no avail.

Later that afternoon, I went to a required group exercise session in chair yoga. They started with clanging the bell and doing other things supposedly to "center" us. I participated in the exercises, but resisted the suggestions being made of what to think about. Instead I was thinking about the Lord and all He had done for me over the past two months. After the session, the instructor volunteered to accompany me back to my room. All the way back, I was asking the Lord what to say to her. Then when we arrived, I just stood there looking at her for a moment with her staring back waiting for me to speak. Finally, I opened my mouth and my personal testimony came out. She listened, but then defended what she was teaching through her yoga session with the usual line of, "Oh, it's just exercise." I suggested that there were any number of other faiths in the hospital and that maybe she thought it was just exercise, but there were others like myself who disagreed with her. So, she said thanks for bringing that to her attention, and that perhaps she should preface her sessions with a statement acknowledging that there were other faiths represented and that participants should feel free to think whatever they wanted during the session.

As soon as she left my room, a housekeeper arrived. Our conversation revolved around the fact that she had recently started reading the Bible looking for direction. I asked her if she knew what would happen to her if she died that day. As often was the case, we were interrupted and were not able to continue our conversation. I never saw her again in my room.

Later that evening, I was speaking on the phone with a sister from church when a patient wheeled herself into my room. Her attendant was a good 50 feet or so behind her and unable to stop her from entering my room. The patient said to me, "You're not a patient here." I replied, "Yes, I am." She came back with, "No, you're not." So I asked, "O.K., who do you think I am?" Her reply was, "You are a friend." So, I said, "Yes, I am a friend, but I am a patient, too." At that moment her attendant caught up with her and tried to remove her from my room, but she made such a fuss. I said to my sister on the phone, "Shelly, please pray now." Then I said to the attendant, "I'm going to pray for your patient." As I prayed, the patient became very quiet and still until she heard the closing of my prayer, "In Jesus' name," at which she had a violent reaction and quickly wheeled herself out of my room. I believed this patient was being influenced by an evil spirit. During the rest of my days in this hospital, whenever I passed her in the hallway, she would look away.

Finally, that evening, the patient wheeled herself into my room again. This time my nurse came and took her out. After she had gone, my nurse returned. I told her that I'd prayed for the patient and she had become agitated. Then I asked my nurse if she knew Jesus. She replied that she was a Jehovah's Witness. She then went into her presentation about her faith. Afterwards, I said, "You and I come from very different belief systems, but may I pray with you?" She replied, "No. I do not allow the opposition to pray with me." With that statement, she left my room.

So many people with so many needs, but all of them need a word from the Lord. We are His mouth piece and it is up to us to speak. I know from experience now what Scripture means when it says in Matthew 10:19-20, "…do not worry about how or what you should speak. For it will be given to you in that hour what you should speak; for it is not you who speak, but the Spirit of your Father who speaks in you." Although this passage was talking about when Jesus was sending out his disciples and he was telling them what to expect if they should be arrested, the principle is the same. When we ask the Holy Spirit to be in control of our lives, we can be confident that when we open our mouths to speak, His words will come out.

^   ^   ^   ^   ^   ^   ^   ^   ^   ^   ^   ^   ^   ^   ^

We are so grateful for our church family who were diligent in praying for us and providing encouraging visits whenever we felt discouraged. For example, one Sunday afternoon about 12 people came down to have a little service with us outside of the hospital in a garden patio area. We sang some songs and shared from the Word. It was very refreshing. Later that evening, Bernie and I went back outside to the patio. There was a young lady covered in tattoos. She was a patient because we saw her arm band. Our conversation turned to the Lord and she revealed that she had just become a Christian a short time ago during her hospitalization. We felt impressed to get a Bible for her. So, we called our "go to" sister from church to find a Bible that we could give to this young lady. Our sister, Pat, 85 years old, got into her car and drove to the local Christian book store, where she used her birthday coupon to purchase a beautiful Bible for this young lady. When we gave it to her, she was overwhelmed. The young lady's mother later told us that was the nicest thing anyone had ever done for her daughter. We continue to pray for this young lady who has a tough road ahead of her. We are also very thankful that our church body has demonstrated ministry to us time and time again.

7
COMING HOME

Update on Barbara's condition Saturday, April 12, 2014 @ 10 p.m. "So the people served the LORD all the days of Joshua, and all the days of the elders who outlived Joshua, who had seen all the great works of the LORD which He had done for Israel. When all that generation had been gathered to their fathers, another generation arose after them who did not know the LORD nor the work which He had done for Israel." Judges 2:7, 10 (NKJV). Good evening Everyone,   On April 10, 2014, Barbara was discharged from the rehab hospital. She spent a total of 73 days in hospital care. God truly worked a miracle in her life. We were told she had Acute Respiratory Distress Syndrome which is something many people do not recover from. It is really insignificant what her condition was; all we know is that God was not finished with her yet. We never want to lose sight of what God was doing in our lives during the past 73 days. **"Then Jesus, being filled with the Holy Spirit, returned from the Jordan and was led by the Spirit into the wilderness, being tempted for forty days by the devil." Luke 4:1-2 (NKJV).** "Extraordinary afflictions are not always the punishment of extraordinary sins, but sometimes the trial of extraordinary graces. God hath many sharp-cutting instruments, and rough files for the polishing of His jewels; and those He especially loves, and means the most resplendent, He hath oftenest His tools upon." Archbishop Leighton.

Now comes the hard part. She needs to continue to exercise her muscles so she can regain her stamina and strength. She's using a walker to get around the house and also to take short excursions out of the house. We also have a wheelchair for her to use when she gets tired of walking. By the time we get through this phase of our recovery, we both should be in pretty good shape. It sure is wonderful to have her home again.   We wish to thank each of you for all your thoughts and prayers over the past couple of months. Now that Barbara's complete recovery is in sight, we will continue to earnestly seek God's direction for our lives. Barbara has begun reading all her condition updates along with all your email responses. If anyone wishes to express their thoughts concerning the past 73 days, please feel free to do so. We would both appreciate reading all your responses. In His Grip, Barbara and Bernie

Philippians 1:6: "being confident of this: that He who began a good work in you shall carry it on to completion, until the day of Christ Jesus".

∧   ∧   ∧   ∧   ∧   ∧   ∧   ∧   ∧   ∧   ∧   ∧   ∧   ∧   ∧

What a difference being out of the hospital has made. I got out two days ago. They would not release me until I could get into my own vehicle. In the process of trying to get into the van, I injured my left arm. So now therapy is in order.

It was so good to get home. We filled our days with concentrating on getting well. Bernie cooked delicious, healthy food, and our neighbor, Margaret, a retired nurse, came over often to check on us. In the evenings, we would take the wheelchair and walker down to a jetty on the beach where we would walk out and enjoy the fresh ocean air and the scenery. We went from a constant stream of individuals coming in and out of the room, to whole days where we just saw each other. Sometimes, I believe, that when a patient is released from the hospital, all those faithful hospital visitors breathe a sigh of relief that their prayers have been answered and now the patient is home. Then they stop visiting! That was a bit of a shock to me. So, the Lord was gracious to me and brought the entire women's Bible study group over to meet in my home. I was very humbled and grateful for these ladies who had unwaveringly prayed for me for the two and one half months I was in the hospital.

^　^　^　^　^　^　^　^　^　^　^　^　^　^　^

Update on Barbara's condition Saturday, May 10, 2014
"Simon Peter said to them, "I am going fishing." They said to him, "We are going with you also." They went out and immediately got into a boat, and that night they caught nothing." John 21:3 (NKJV).　Good evening Everyone,　Today marks the one month anniversary of Barbara's discharge from the hospital. Her condition continues to improve. Her strength and stamina are slowly coming back to her, with the help of a visiting physical therapist who has been coming to the house 2-3 times a week over the last month. Next, she will receive therapy through an outpatient rehab facility.　At present, she is walking around the house unassisted. Often, we go out either in the evening or early morning to a cool location and she will walk a short distance using a walker and/or a wheel chair. We still have some small issues we have to deal with, but all in all, life is good and we are truly grateful to God for His great mercy and grace He has poured out on us over these last few months. And we are grateful for all your thoughts and prayers on our behalf.

You may be wondering why we chose the above passage from John to introduce this letter. A very traumatic event had recently taken place in the disciple's lives, [the crucifixion and resurrection of the Lord], and their reaction was to return to their former way of life. But Jesus showed up, and He assured them that their lives would never be the same again. We believe God brought this traumatic situation into our lives to redirect our lives. We pray that His Presence will direct us in the way He wants us to go; never again to return to our former way of life. Thanks again for your thoughts and prayers.
In His Grip,   Barbara & Bernie

Bernie, We all were in a very dark cloud during Barbara's unexpected illness. I honestly thought she was going to "visit our grandparents," but then, a miracle happened. God is amazing! This experience has truly restored my faith. Bernie, I have to commend you for constantly being at my cousin's side, and making sure she had the best care, and for all your praying. I'm sure your knees are still recovering. Thank you for your daily updates and Scriptures. Barbara, we are so happy and blessed to have you back. We pray for a full and speedy recovery! Love you!!   Sandy

8
REFLECTIONS

Sometime in the early days after I came home, Bernie hit a wall. He had been surviving on adrenaline for so long, and suddenly it left him overnight. Bernie became distant toward me. I couldn't understand what was happening. I didn't say anything for a while because, understandably, he had been through more emotionally than I had. Later he related to me that he felt like he was alone, but that he was determined that he was going to keep his faith in God intact. He isolated himself and cried out to the Lord, "Where are you now? I need you now!" He also said, "Lord, I don't sense your presence, but I know you are here. Help me get through this time." In the past, whenever we have gone through difficult times, we have not always seen the Lord's presence in the difficulties, but when we have emerged on the other side, we have been able to look back and realize God was there all along supporting us.

This incident reminds me of one in Scripture. In 1 Kings 17-19, we read the account of Elijah the prophet, and his encounter with the prophets of Baal. Elijah had prophesied that there would be a drought. During the beginning days of the drought, God supplied Elijah with water from a brook, and the ravens supplied food for him. When the brook dried up, God sent him to a widow who provided for his needs. Meanwhile, Jezebel was killing off the prophets while Obadiah was preserving some of them by hiding them in caves. It was at this time that Elijah met the prophets of Baal at Mount Carmel. Elijah challenged the people to return to serve the Lord and reject Baal, but the people did not respond. So Elijah proposed a show down between the prophets of Baal and himself, the prophet of God. The prophets of Baal failed to produce fire to consume their sacrifices, but God, at Elijah's request, sent a mighty fire to consume not only the sacrifice Elijah had presented, but the sacrifices of Baal as well. The prophets of Baal were then slaughtered as the people realized God was indeed God! After this event, the rain returned. Of course, Jezebel was not happy about this turn of events, so she threatened Elijah with death. Elijah was afraid and he ran for his life. He laid down under a broom tree and prayed all night that he would die. He said in **1 Kings 19:4: "I have had enough, LORD. Take my life; I am no better than my ancestors."** This was the desperate prayer of an exhausted man who had witnessed a mighty working of the Lord God through himself as the vessel. Apparently, sleep and nourishment were needed. God sent an angel to provide food and water and Elijah went to sleep again. A second time, the angel returned and provided food and water. This time he was able to travel 40 days and nights to Horeb. It was here the word of the Lord came to him. Elijah complained that he had been very zealous for the Lord, but the Israelites had rejected the Lord, and now they were trying to kill him as well. Shortly after this, the Lord communicated to Elijah again. A change was coming.

Bernie had been through unbelievable strain on his emotions and was at the point of emotional collapse. I am grateful the Lord did not let him stay in this state, but, like Elijah, refreshed him and restored him to stand.

In conclusion, the church is a body of believers, and when one member hurts, we all hurt. We have learned so much from this hospitalization experience and pray that it will continue to make us changed persons. We want our lives to be invested in those things that will survive our physical bodies: God, His Word, and people.

ABOUT THE AUTHORS

Husband and wife, Barbara K. Black and Bernard F. Black, have served the Lord through their local churches for more than 37 years. They particularly enjoy working with international students teaching them to speak English as a Second Language. They also pursue music, photography, and travel. This account of Barbara's hospitalization put the couple's faith to a test much like the refining process rids gold of impurities. Come along and relive this journey with them.

www.ingramcontent.com/pod-product-compliance
Lightning Source LLC
Chambersburg PA
CBHW070528030426
42337CB00016B/2154